**W9-DFG-037**

# Immigration Policy

## Second Edition

# Immigration Policy
## Second Edition

By Alan Allport and John E. Ferguson Jr.

SERIES CONSULTING EDITOR
Alan Marzilli, M.A., J.D.

CHELSEA HOUSE
P U B L I S H E R S
An imprint of Infobase Publishing

**Immigration Policy, Second Edition**

Chelsea House
An imprint of Infobase Publishing
132 West 31st Street
New York NY 10001

**Library of Congress Cataloging-in-Publication Data**

Allport, Alan, 1970-
   Immigration policy / by Alan Allport.—2nd ed. / rev. by John E. Ferguson, Jr.
      p. cm.—(Point/counterpoint)
   Includes bibliographical references and index.
   ISBN 978-1-60413-126-0 (hardcover)
   1. United States—Emigration and immigration—Government policy—Juvenile literature. 2. English-only movement—United States—Juvenile literature. 3. English language—Political aspects—United States—Juvenile literature. 4. Language policy—United States—Juvenile literature. I. Ferguson, John E. II. Title. III. Series.
   JV6483.A437 2009
   325.73—dc22                                        2008035049

Chelsea House books are available at special discounts when purchased in bulk quantities for businesses, associations, institutions, or sales promotions. Please call our Special Sales Department in New York at (212) 967-8800 or (800) 322-8755.

You can find Chelsea House on the World Wide Web at
http://www.chelseahouse.com

Series design by Keith Trego
Cover design by Keith Trego and Alicia Post

Printed in the United States of America

Bang NMSG 10 9 8 7 6 5 4 3 2 1

This book is printed on acid-free paper.

All links and Web addresses were checked and verified to be correct at the time of publication. Because of the dynamic nature of the Web, some addresses and links may have changed since publication and may no longer be valid.

POINT |||
◀|||||COUNTERPOINT

33.95

# *FOREWORD* ⫻▷

**Alan Marzilli, M.A., J.D.**
**Birmingham, Alabama**

The POINT/COUNTERPOINT series offers the reader a greater understanding of some of the most controversial issues in contemporary
American society—issues such as capital punishment, immigration,
gay rights, and gun control. We have looked for the most contemporary issues and have included topics—such as the controversies
surrounding "blogging"—that we could not have imagined when the
series began.

In each volume, the author has selected an issue of particular
importance and set out some of the key arguments on both sides of the
issue. Why study both sides of the debate? Maybe you have yet to make
up your mind on an issue, and the arguments presented in the book
will help you to form an opinion. More likely, however, you will already
have an opinion on many of the issues covered by the series. There is
always the chance that you will change your opinion after reading the
arguments for the other side. But even if you are firmly committed to
an issue—for example, school prayer or animal rights—reading both
sides of the argument will help you to become a more effective advocate for your cause. By gaining an understanding of opposing arguments, you can develop answers to those arguments.

Perhaps more importantly, listening to the other side sometimes
helps you see your opponent's arguments in a more human way. For
example, Sister Helen Prejean, one of the nation's most visible opponents of capital punishment, has been deeply affected by her interac-
tions with the families of murder victims. By seeing the families' grief
and pain, she understands much better why people support the death
penalty, and she is able to carry out her advocacy with a greater sensi-
tivity to the needs and beliefs of death penalty supporters.

The books in the series include numerous features that help the
reader to gain a greater understanding of the issues. Real-life examples
illustrate the human side of the issues. Each chapter also includes
excerpts from relevant laws, court cases, and other material, which
provide a better foundation for understanding the arguments. The

volumes contain citations to relevant sources of law and information, and an appendix guides the reader through the basics of legal research, both on the Internet and in the library. Today, through free Web sites, it is easy to access legal documents, and these books might give you ideas for your own research.

Studying the issues covered by the POINT/COUNTERPOINT series is more than an academic activity. The issues described in the book affect all of us as citizens. They are the issues that today's leaders debate and tomorrow's leaders will decide. While all of the issues covered in the POINT/COUNTERPOINT series are controversial today, and will remain so for the foreseeable future, it is entirely possible that the reader might one day play a central role in resolving the debate. Today it might seem that some debates—such as capital punishment and abortion—will never be resolved.

However, our nation's history is full of debates that seemed as though they never would be resolved, and many of the issues are now well settled—at least on the surface. In the nineteenth century, abolitionists met with widespread resistance to their efforts to end slavery. Ultimately, the controversy threatened the union, leading to the Civil War between the northern and southern states. Today, while a public debate over the merits of slavery would be unthinkable, racism persists in many aspects of society.

Similarly, today nobody questions women's right to vote. Yet at the beginning of the twentieth century, suffragists fought public battles for women's voting rights, and it was not until the passage of the Nineteenth Amendment in 1920 that the legal right of women to vote was established nationwide.

What makes an issue controversial? Often, controversies arise when most people agree that there is a problem, but people disagree about the best way to solve the problem. There is little argument that poverty is a major problem in the United States, especially in inner cities and rural areas. Yet, people disagree vehemently about the best way to address the problem. To some, the answer is social programs, such as welfare, food stamps, and public housing. However, many argue that such subsidies encourage dependence on government benefits while unfairly penalizing those who work and pay taxes, and that the real solution is to require people to support themselves.

American society is in a constant state of change, and sometimes modern practices clash with what many consider to be "traditional values," which are often rooted in conservative political views or religious beliefs. Many blame high crime rates, and problems such as poverty, illiteracy, and drug use on the breakdown of the traditional family structure of a married mother and father raising their children. Since the "sexual revolution" of the 1960s and 1970s, sparked in part by the widespread availability of the birth control pill, marriage rates have declined, and the number of children born outside of marriage has increased. The sexual revolution led to controversies over birth control, sex education, and other issues, most prominently abortion. Similarly, the gay rights movement has been challenged as a threat to traditional values. While many gay men and lesbians want to have the same right to marry and raise families as heterosexuals, many politicians and others have challenged gay marriage and adoption as a threat to American society.

Sometimes, new technology raises issues that we have never faced before, and society disagrees about the best solution. Are people free to swap music online, or does this violate the copyright laws that protect songwriters and musicians' ownership of the music that they create? Should scientists use "genetic engineering" to create new crops that are resistant to disease and pests and produce more food, or is it too risky to use a laboratory to create plants that nature never intended? Modern medicine has continued to increase the average lifespan—which is now 77 years, up from under 50 years at the beginning of the twentieth century—but many people are now choosing to die in comfort rather than living with painful ailments in their later years. For doctors, this presents an ethical dilemma: should they allow their patients to die? Should they assist patients in ending their own lives painlessly?

Perhaps the most controversial issues are those that implicate a Constitutional right. The Bill of Rights—the first 10 Amendments to the U.S. Constitution—spell out some of the most fundamental rights that distinguish our democracy from other nations with fewer freedoms. However, the sparsely worded document is open to interpretation, with each side saying that the Constitution is on their side. The Bill of Rights was meant to protect individual liberties; however, the needs of some individuals clash with society's needs. Thus, the Constitution often serves as a battleground between individuals and government officials seeking to protect society in some way. The First Amendment's guarantee of "freedom of speech" leads to some very difficult questions. Some forms of expression—such as burning an American flag—lead to public outrage, but are protected by the First Amendment. Other types of expression that most people find objectionable—such as child pornography—are not protected by the Constitution. The question is not only where to draw the line, but whether drawing lines around constitutional rights threatens our liberty.

The Bill of Rights raises many other questions about individual rights and societal "good." Is a prayer before a high school football game an "establishment of religion" prohibited by the First Amendment? Does the Second Amendment's promise of "the right to bear arms" include concealed handguns? Does stopping and frisking someone standing on a known drug corner constitute "unreasonable search and seizure" in violation of the Fourth Amendment? Although the U.S. Supreme Court has the ultimate authority in interpreting the U.S. Constitution, their answers do not always satisfy the public. When a group of nine people—sometimes by a five-to-four vote—makes a decision that affects hundreds of millions of others, public outcry can be expected. For example, the Supreme Court's 1973 ruling in *Roe v. Wade* that abortion is protected by the Constitution did little to quell the debate over abortion.

Whatever the root of the controversy, the books in the POINT/ COUNTERPOINT series seek to explain to the reader both the origins of the debate, the current state of the law, and the arguments on either side of the debate. Our hope in creating this series is that the reader will be better informed about the issues facing not only our politicians, but all of our nation's citizens, and become more actively involved in resolving these debates, as voters, concerned citizens, journalists, or maybe even elected officials.

This expanded and updated edition of *Immigration Policy* looks at controversies surrounding immigration, both legal and illegal. Many have described the United States as a "melting pot," in which people from many foreign places, with their own languages and cultures, have formed a society with great diversity. The work ethic and entrepreneurial spirit of generations of immigrants have helped the United States become a global economic and cultural leader. However, many worry that allowing unchecked immigration drains the U.S. economy and places burdens on its citizens.

New to this edition is an examination of the controversies surrounding the ongoing effort to build a wall along the United States' southern border with Mexico. Many of the arguments relating to this controversy are racially charged, as there has been no effort to build a wall along the northern border with Canada. However, arguments over the wall also reflect some of the economic arguments related to both legal and illegal immigrants, which this volume discusses in detail. As the Latino population increases and Spanish language media, advertising, and commercial and government services proliferate, some have pushed for English to be made the official language of the United States.

# A Scene from American Life

I t takes place in a large room. It could be a courtroom, a civic center, or any of thousands of places across the United States where such events happen every week. For our purposes, let us assume it is in a library in the city of Dorchester, Massachusetts. The room is filled with several hundred men, women, and children of different ages, races, and religions. A lot of the people in the room are there as friends, colleagues, and bystanders, but for 194 of those present, the day marks a turning point in their lives. They are about to take the final step before becoming official citizens of the United States of America.

For some of those 194, particularly those who came from modern democracies such as Canada, the United Kingdom, or Australia, the moment of becoming an American citizen might not seem all that significant. They may have come to the United States just to work or for family or private reasons, and

**11**

they originate from countries not all that different culturally or politically from the United States. The decision to take an American passport—to become "naturalized" citizens, in the jargon of immigration law—may have been a practical one, an administrative chore without any great personal meaning. For others, especially those from less-fortunate backgrounds, the consequences of naturalization are much more profound. These people may have been born in countries with oppressive governments, such as China, or else have escaped from war-torn regions such as Somalia. Perhaps they arrived in the United States as penniless, homeless refugees, speaking no English and unsure whether they would be allowed to stay or what their futures would hold. Many of them have spent years, or even decades, working painstakingly toward the goal of naturalization. To them, accepting American citizenship is a lot more than a bureaucratic nicety. It represents the end of an uncertain life full of frightening episodes and the promise of rebirth in a country rich with opportunity and democratic ideals. The moment is exciting: "This freedom is so wonderful, I can feel it in the air," says one, an Iranian student who as a child was forced to flee her hometown when Saddam Hussein's Iraqi forces invaded in 1980 and who has waited many years for this day.

The federal judge leading the afternoon's ceremony announces to the crowd that it is time to take the Oath of Allegiance to the United States, which is legally required of every naturalizing citizen. Together, the assembly rises, everyone raises his or her right hand, and all recite as one:

> I hereby declare, on oath, that I absolutely and entirely renounce and abjure all allegiance and fidelity to any foreign prince, potentate, state, or sovereignty, of whom or which I have heretofore been a subject or citizen; that I will support and defend the Constitution and laws of the United States of America against all enemies, foreign and domestic; that I will bear true faith and allegiance to the same; that I will bear

arms on behalf of the United States when required by the law; that I will perform noncombatant service in the Armed Forces of the United States when required by the law; that I will perform work of national importance under civilian direction when required by the law; and that I take this obligation freely, without any mental reservation or purpose of evasion; so help me God.[1]

After this is completed, to the accompaniment of cheers, laughter, and many tears, the 194 new citizens receive their official certificates of naturalization and repeat the traditional Pledge of Allegiance for the first time. They are no longer Germans, Pakistanis, Argentineans, or Sudanese; they are citizens of the United States of America.[2]

## America and Immigration

The story of these modern Massachusetts pilgrims is typical of American history. The United States was founded as, and has remained for more than 200 years, a land of immigration. Some of the people reading this book were born outside the United States, and many more have at least one parent, grandparent, or great-grandparent who was born in another country. With the exception of the small Native American population, *everyone* living in the United States can trace his or her ancestry back to immigrants, whether they came from Europe, South or Central America, Asia, Africa, or some other part of the world; whether they traveled here willingly or were forced to come by the hand of slavery; and whether they found their new American home to be a land of plenty or of disappointment and bitterness. The experience of immigration binds almost every modern American citizen in a common heritage.

From its first days, America was a rich confluence of races, languages, and creeds. In its early history, the United States had three main sources of immigration. The first were the European colonists who built the string of coastal towns and provinces along the Atlantic seaboard that eventually became the United States; most of these people were originally from the countries of the British Isles—England, Scotland, Ireland, and Wales—as well as the French settlers of "Acadia," or Newfoundland, who eventually ended up in Louisiana. Second were the African slaves who were forcibly brought to the Southern colonies to work on tobacco and cotton plantations and who had to wait until the Civil War of 1861–1865 to win freedom. Third were Hispanic migrants—people whose ancestry was a mixture of Spanish and Native American—who moved northward from Mexico to settle in what are now states such as California, Florida, and Texas.

Throughout the nineteenth century, the immigration story became even more complex. Millions of Europeans—Irish, Germans, Swedes, Poles, Russians, and Italians, among many other nationalities—journeyed across the Atlantic to America. On the West Coast, Chinese workers began to arrive in large numbers to serve as itinerant laborers in the booming Gold Rush towns of California. Migration from Mexico continued at a fast rate. Over time, some of these groups settled in particular city districts and formed communities with distinct linguistic and cultural identities, such as Chinatown in San Francisco and New York's Little Italy.

As America's ethnic mixture became ever more intricate, some people from the "WASP" (White Anglo-Saxon Protestant) elite that traditionally held much of the power and wealth became concerned about the "dilution" of the country's population as a result of the influx of foreign peoples and ideas—a form of polite and not-so-polite bigotry that would turn into an important political force under the so-called "nativist" banner. It was the demands of nativists, as well as public concerns about crime, health, and unemployment, that encouraged the federal government to introduce comprehensive immigration laws and controls around the end of the nineteenth century.

The 1882 Immigration Act was the nation's first major attempt to define who could or could not legally enter the United

## Census 2000: Foreign Speakers Increase

More people spoke a language other than English at home in 2000 than in 1990. More people also spoke English less than "very well."

**1990**

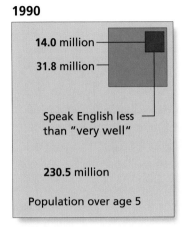

14.0 million
31.8 million

Speak English less than "very well"

230.5 million

Population over age 5

**2000**

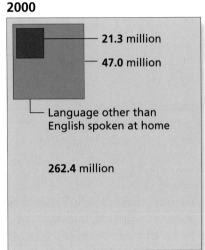

21.3 million
47.0 million

Language other than English spoken at home

262.4 million

*Source:* Census Bureau
© Infobase Publishing

Immigration has been a part of American life since the founding of the nation, but the face of immigration has constantly changed. The most recent census taken in 2000 found a significant increase in foreign language speakers in the United States, as well as an increase in foreign language speakers who are able to speak English less than "very well."

States. The act levied a head tax of 50 cents on every immigrant and formally barred the immigration of "idiots, lunatics, convicts, and persons likely to become a public charge."[3] The same year, Congress also passed the Chinese Exclusion Act, which outlawed emigration from China to the United States on the grounds that "the coming of Chinese laborers to this country endangers the good order"—although the new law really had more to do with competition for low-wage jobs in California.[4] This act, the first attempt by the government to bar the immigration of a specific national or racial group, was part of American law for more than 60 years and was not repealed until World War II.

In 1891, another immigration act broadened the category of persons forbidden to enter the United States to include polygamists, previously convicted criminals, and those suffering from contagious diseases. It also created the Office of the Superintendent of Immigration, the first of many federal departments responsible for the regulation of people coming into the country and the forerunner of today's U.S. Citizenship and Immigration Services, or USCIS. Part of the new

## THE LETTER OF THE LAW

## Extracts from the 1952 Immigration and Nationality Act (Amended)

ALLOCATION OF IMMIGRANT VISAS: Sec. 203. [8 U.S.C. 1153]

(a) Preference Allocation for Family-Sponsored Immigrants.—Aliens subject to the worldwide level specified in section 201(c) for family-sponsored immigrants shall be allotted visas as follows:

(1) Unmarried sons and daughters of citizens.—Qualified immigrants who are the unmarried sons or daughters of citizens of the United States shall be allocated visas in a number not to exceed 23,400 ... (2) Spouses and unmarried sons and unmarried daughters of permanent resident aliens ... (3) Married sons and married daughters of citizens ... (4) Brothers and sisters of citizens ...

(b) Preference Allocation for Employment-Based Immigrants.—Aliens subject to the worldwide level specified in section 201(d) for employment-based immigrants in a fiscal year shall be allotted visas as follows:

(1) Priority workers—aliens described in any of the following subparagraphs (A) through (C):

superintendent's job was to manage a number of immigration-control depots set up at important ports and cities around the United States, the most famous of which was Ellis Island, situated in the middle of New York Harbor. Ellis Island opened on January 2, 1892, and in the 62 years in which it operated, more than 12 million immigrants passed through the facility's famous registry room, awaiting entry into the United States; more than 100 million Americans today can trace their ancestry to someone who disembarked from an immigrant ship at Ellis Island.

The years 1890 to the early 1920s were the peak period of immigration to the United States. After the United States entered World War I in 1917, there was strong political pressure to reduce the number of foreign-born persons in the country.

(A) Aliens with extraordinary ability ... the alien has extraordinary ability in the sciences, arts, education, business, or athletics which has been demonstrated by sustained national or international acclaim and whose achievements have been recognized in the field through extensive documentation ... (B) Outstanding professors and researchers ... (C) Certain multinational executives and managers ...
(2) Aliens who are members of the professions holding advanced degrees or aliens of exceptional ability ...
(3) Skilled workers, professionals, and other workers ...
(c) Diversity Immigrants ...
Requirement of education or work experience.—An alien is not eligible for a visa under this subsection unless the alien—
(A) has at least a high school education or its equivalent, or
(B) has, within 5 years of the date of application for a visa under this subsection, at least 2 years of work experience in an occupation which requires at least 2 years of training or experience ...

Source: 1952 Immigration and Nationality Act (Amended). Available online at: http://www.uscis.gov/propub/ProPubVAP.jsp?dockey=cb90c19a50729fb47fb0686648558dbe

Congress responded with a series of laws making it increasingly difficult to enter the United States legally. For the first time, would-be immigrants had to be able to read and write in their native language or else were considered too "intellectually inferior" to qualify for entry. This was a considerable hurdle: Even as late as World War I, the majority of people from largely peasant societies such as Sicily and Poland were illiterate.

Another complication was added in 1924, when the government introduced a national-origins quota system, which fixed a numerical limit on the number of immigrants from any single country who could enter. Because the quotas were based on the ethnic mix of the American population at the time, people who originated from outside Europe found it much harder to immigrate than Europeans. Given these restrictions, it is not surprising that total immigration numbers fell sharply from the 1920s on.

During the next three decades, Congress made a series of changes to the country's immigration laws, making them increasingly difficult to understand, even for professionals responsible for implementing them. To try to remedy this, in 1952, Congress passed the Immigration and Nationality Act, which brought all the existing regulations together in one coherent form and remains to this day the basis of American immigration law. (Unfortunately, in the half-century since it was introduced, this act has itself been amended many times, which means that its admirable simplicity is now mostly a fond memory.)

Until 1965, the national-origins quota system was the chief means of deciding which immigrants could enter the United States. By the mid-1960s, complaints that this method was arbitrary and even racist led to a complete rethink of the way immigration was handled. The result was the preference system, which abandoned quotas by nationality and instead created two "privileged" categories of immigrants: those who were related to American citizens by family or marriage and those who had special technical or educational skills that were useful to the

American economy. Potential immigrants who did not fall into either of these categories now found it much harder to permanently enter the United States, regardless of where they originally came from. Preference continues to be used as the main method of allocating immigration visas today.

## Basic Facts About Immigration Today

That is the historical context of America's immigration policy. How does the system work in the twenty-first century? This is a complex subject, particularly as one expert has described American immigration procedures as "a body of laws which are inconsistent, contradictory and unguided by any central theme."[5]

Anyone present in the United States who is not a citizen is considered an "alien." This term has nothing to do with green skin or ray guns, but simply means a person with a foreign passport, or no passport at all. The Census Bureau estimates that 37.9 million aliens currently live in the United States.[6]

Every alien must, by law, possess some kind of visa in order to enter the country. The two principal kinds of visa are "nonimmigrant" and "immigrant." Nonimmigrant visas allow aliens to enter the United States for *a fixed period of time only*, a few months to several years, and often on the condition that they perform a certain job or study at a certain institution. There are several ways in which an alien can receive a nonimmigrant visa; they range from tourism—which usually allows a person to stay in the country for three months but forbids him or her from working during that period—to studying at an American university or working for an American employer. The different types of nonimmigrant visa are known by a letter code: "F," "M," and "J" visas are for students, for example, and "H" is for temporary workers. By law, the government can allocate only a fixed number of certain types of letter-coded visa every year. For example, "U" visas for alien victims of crimes are limited to 10,000 each year.[7]

The exact conditions attached to individual nonimmigrant visas vary a lot, but the key that connects them is that they do not allow their holders to live *permanently* in the United States or to become American citizens. A nonimmigrant visa is a short-term permit only, and anyone who holds one is expected to leave the United States and return to his or her home country. If he or she does not do so before the visa expires, the person becomes an "illegal alien" subject to deportation (addressed later in this text). All visitors from countries other than Mexico and Canada are required to apply for their visa by using the I-94 form. Certain high-frequency visitors from Mexico and Canada have separate procedures for requesting a visa. In 2006, approximately 33.7 million aliens received nonimmigrant visas through the I-94 system and 141 million Mexican and Canadian visitors entered through other systems. Of the I-94 visitors, 89% were in the U.S. for short-term vacations and business trips.[8]

Someone who would like to enter the United States for good and establish a permanent home here must first get an immigrant visa. These are allocated only under special conditions, and a person who wishes to receive one must fall into one of the preference categories mentioned in the previous section. The two most important categories are "family sponsored" and "employment sponsored." Family-sponsored immigration is possible only if an alien is married to or is a close blood relative of an American citizen. Because of the potential for abuse of the system, alien spouses must prove that they have a bona fide relationship with their wife or husband and have not entered a so-called "sham marriage" simply to get around the immigration rules. Some of these family sponsorships are subject to annual limits in the same way as nonimmigrant visas, but others are unlimited.

An immigration visa on employment grounds is much more difficult to obtain than "H"-type nonimmigrant working papers: The applicant must prove that he or she has truly exceptional skills vital to the American workforce and that few or no American citizen possess such skills to the same degree. Often, these are people who work in health care or technology industries, or who are academics.

Two other ways of receiving an immigrant visa emerged recently. In the early 1990s, Congress introduced the "diversity" category, sometimes known as the "green card lottery," which allocates visas to people of certain nationalities that traditionally are underrepresented in the immigrant pool. To receive a diversity visa, all an eligible candidate has to do is apply for one. The number available in any given year is very limited, however, which is why the process resembles a lottery. The other important preference category is for refugees and asylum seekers, the largest numbers of which come from Cuba.

How many immigrant visas are awarded each year? In 2006, 1,052,415 new applications were approved; of these, about 689,820 were on grounds of family sponsorship, 162,176 were employer sponsored, 42,127 were in the diversity category, and 136,125 were refugees or others seeking asylum. Some of these visas were awarded to aliens newly arrived from outside the United States, and others—so-called "adjustments"—went to people already present in the United States as nonimmigrants, such as aliens who married American citizens while they were studying on "F"-type visas.[9]

Persons who receive immigrant visas—"resident aliens"— are *not* American citizens; they cannot vote, serve on juries, or run for public office. They do, however, enjoy the civil rights protections of the U.S. Constitution, and they are free to live and work anywhere in the country without restriction. As proof of their special status, they are given small plastic ID cards officially called "Alien Registration Receipt Cards," but universally known as "green cards." This nickname refers to the color of the original cards, which have long since been replaced; green cards are no longer green—the current ones are pink. Possession of a green card is an important privilege, and it often takes months, or even years, to obtain one.

For some immigrants, being a resident alien in the United States is a satisfactory condition that allows them to live without any major problems, and they retain their foreign nationality for life, even if they never return to their home countries. For others, however, the ultimate goal is to acquire American citizenship. The process for doing this is called "naturalization." Normally, to be eligible for naturalization in the United States, a person must hold resident alien status for three to five years, depending on the exact circumstances; have no criminal convictions or other black marks on his or her character; and permanently maintain a home address within the United States. Applicants must also undertake an English comprehension exam, a simple test of their knowledge of American history and culture, and make a formal oath of allegiance to the United States at a ceremony like the one described at the beginning of this chapter. Some aliens must surrender their old passports after naturalization, whereas others (depending on their country of origin) can maintain "dual nationality" and be citizens of the United States as well as their place of birth. In 2006, 702,589 former aliens were naturalized as Americans.[10]

Any alien within American borders who does not have a visa, immigrant or nonimmigrant, is here illegally. Illegal aliens are of two types: persons who enter the country legitimately as tourists or other visa holders and then do not leave when their paperwork expires, and those who illicitly cross the Canadian or Mexican land frontiers or stow away on incoming planes or ships. Lacking Social Security numbers or proper papers, such aliens are ineligible to work in the United States, although many get jobs in the so-called "underground economy" with the tacit knowledge of their employers. Illegal aliens who are apprehended by the government are usually deported and often are placed on a permanent record that prevents them from reentering the United States, even on otherwise legal grounds. By the very nature of illegal immigrants' status, it is very difficult to obtain a reliable figure of how many are present in the United States at any given time. In 2006, the federal authorities located 1,206,457 people who were subject to deportation because they lacked appropriate visas; it has been estimated that there are at least 11.3 million illegal aliens now residing in the United States.[11]

## Current Controversies

Immigrants to the United States have always conjured up a wide range of images and provoked very different responses from native-born Americans. To some, they are the "tired, poor, huddled masses" of Emma Lazarus's famous poem engraved on the base of the Statue of Liberty, the "wretched refuse of the teeming shore" who have fled the corrupt Old World to come to the New and whose plight should provoke sympathy and charity in American hearts. According to this view, the United States, an affluent and powerful nation that built its wealth with the hard work of

## "The New Colossus" by Emma Lazarus (1883)

Not like the brazen giant of Greek fame,
with conquering limbs astride from land to land;
Here at our sea-washed, sunset gates shall stand
a mighty woman with a torch, whose flame
is the imprisoned lightning, and her name
Mother of Exiles. From her beacon-hand
Glows world-wide welcome; her mild eyes command
The air-bridged harbor that twin cities frame,
"Keep, ancient lands, your storied pomp!" cries she
with silent lips. "Give me your tired, your poor,
Your huddled masses yearning to breathe free,
The wretched refuse of your teeming shore,
Send these, the homeless, tempest-tost to me,
I lift my lamp beside the golden door!"

Source: http://www.libertystatepark.com/emma.htm

immigrant waves in the past, has a moral responsibility to take in the poor and downtrodden. Under this line of thinking, this is not only an ethical imperative; it makes good sense, too. Immigrants enrich the country both materially and culturally.

The alternative view, no less popular, is that immigration today is at best a necessary burden and at worst a drain on America's fragile resources and a strain on its social fabric. Yes, goes this argument, the United States has traditionally been a land of immigrants—but with a population approaching the 300 million mark and an unusually high birthrate for an industrial nation, this country can no longer afford to take in large

# Extracts from the U.S. Department of Justice Report on the September 11 Detainees

In the aftermath of the September 11 terrorist attacks, the Department of Justice used the federal immigration laws to detain aliens who were suspected of having ties to the attacks or terrorism in general. More than 750 aliens who had violated immigration laws were arrested and detained in connection with the FBI's investigation into the attacks, called PENTTBOM. Our review examined the treatment of these detainees, including their processing, bond decisions, the timing of their removal or release, their access to counsel, and their conditions of confinement....

In conducting our review, we were mindful of the circumstances confronting the Department and the country as a result of the September 11 attacks, including the massive disruptions they caused. The Department was faced with monumental challenges, and Department employees worked tirelessly and with enormous dedication over an extended period to meet these challenges. It is also important to note that nearly all of the 762 aliens we examined violated immigration laws, either by overstaying their visas, by entering the country illegally, or some other immigration violation....

While recognizing the difficult circumstances confronting the Department in responding to the terrorist attacks, we found significant problems in the way the September 11 detainees were treated. The INS did not serve notices of the immigration charges on these detainees within the specified timeframes. This delay

numbers of foreign-born people. There is no longer a western frontier to populate; the country is, in effect, full. Limited immigration on high-skill or compassionate grounds might still be tolerated, but it makes no sense to continue inviting immigrants who cannot be absorbed properly into the country's financial, social, or political life.

Much of this debate centers on the economic effects of immigration, but there is an important cultural component as well. Critics of immigration complain that too many people arrive in the United States with only a limited understanding of the country's history, customs, and way of life—and they stay

affected the detainees in several ways, from their ability to understand why they were being held, to their ability to obtain legal counsel, to their ability to request a bond hearing.

In addition, the Department instituted a policy that these detainees would be held until cleared by the FBI. Although not communicated in writing, this "hold until cleared" policy was clearly understood and applied throughout the Department. The policy was based on the belief—which turned out to be erroneous—that the FBI's clearance process would proceed quickly. Instead of taking a few days as anticipated, the clearance process took an average of 80 days, primarily because it was understaffed and not given sufficient priority by the FBI.

We also found that the FBI and the INS in New York City made little attempt to distinguish between aliens who were subjects of the PENTTBOM investigation and those encountered coincidentally to a PENTTBOM lead. Even in the chaotic aftermath of the September 11 attacks, we believe the FBI should have taken more care to distinguish between aliens who it actually suspected of having a connection to terrorism from those aliens who, while possibly guilty of violating federal immigration law, had no connection to terrorism but simply were encountered in connection with a PENTTBOM lead....

Source: U.S. Department of Justice Office of the Inspector General, *The September 11 Detainees: A Review of the Treatment of Aliens Held on Immigration Charges in Connection with the Investigation of the September 11 Attacks* (2003). Available online at: http://www.usdoj.gov/oig/special/0306/index.htm

that way. In the past, foreign-born citizens shed much of their old identity and adopted an American lifestyle in the so-called "melting pot"; today, critics claim there is increasing resistance to this. The result is a civilization fractured along racial and cultural lines—a process sometimes known as the "balkanization" of society, referring to the peoples of the Balkan region of Southeastern Europe, who are divided by religion, language, and tradition.

One proposed way of preventing this balkanization is to make English the single official language of the United States and to require all of the country's public affairs to be conducted in English alone, proponents say. Opponents of this balkanization theory counterargue that multilingualism has always existed in the United States and that, in any case, the country's cultural heritage gains from the contribution of ideas from outside. They complain that an official language is unnecessary, because nearly all Americans acquire a working knowledge of English and such a rule would be used as a discriminatory tool against minority groups such as those who speak Spanish as a native tongue.

Some have proposed that stopping illegal immigration can be done only by physically securing the borders, especially the border with Mexico. These advocates propose a border wall be built on the U.S. southern border to stem the tide of illegal immigrants. Citizen groups have joined this effort by organizing civilian militias to patrol the border. Critics argue that such physical security measures are ineffective, and that they will lead to environmental and other problems.

These battles over immigration have been going on for decades—some of them are as old as America itself—but the events of September 11, 2001, and the subsequent war on terrorism have cast immigration in a new and worrying light. As it became clear that the hijackers responsible for the 9/11 atrocities were aliens who entered the United States on nonimmigrant visas, some of which were dubiously acquired, the fear arose across the country that lax immigration policy might not present just an economic and cultural challenge but also a security threat. Did America have a foreign-born "enemy within" actively encouraging and sheltering terrorists?

One early repercussion of this fear was that the Immigration and Naturalization Service (INS), which had been in charge of handling immigration issues since 1933 but had been criticized for its bureaucratic muddle, was scrapped. In 2002, the new Department of Homeland Security took over immigration affairs and the old responsibilities of the INS were broken down into a series of replacement federal bodies. The Transportation Security Administration (TSA) is tasked with securing and monitoring everything from highways and airports to shipping ports and mass transit systems. The U.S. Customs and Border Protection (USCBP) and Immigration and Customs Enforcement (ICE) are both designed to investigate and secure borders and enforce customs regulations at airports, shipping centers and other border crossings. Meanwhile, the administration of visa and citizenship inquiries was turned over to U.S. Citizenship and Immigration Services (USCIS). The idea of this breakdown was that the USCIS would be the "polite" face of U.S. immigration law, handling routine, legitimate requests from the public at home and abroad, and the USCBP and ICE would deal with the less genteel problems of monitoring illegal immigration and smuggling. The demise of the INS was little mourned by anyone, but it is too early to tell how successful the new departments will be.

What we do know is that the status of foreign-born residents in American society has become one of the hot-button issues of the twenty-first century. The government has required all aliens with nonimmigrant visas who come from certain countries suspected of harboring terrorists—such as Iran, Sudan, Syria, and Libya—to reregister with the federal authorities and be fingerprinted, photographed, and questioned under oath. Some people complain that these special provisions are a form of racial targeting and are intended to make aliens into convenient scapegoats who can be persecuted because they have no political lobby to defend them. Others say that, on the contrary, the government isn't doing enough to keep an eye on foreign nationals, some of whom are students, possibly with access to sensitive technical and scientific knowledge that could be used by terrorists.

As another example, in the aftermath of 9/11, the Justice Department apprehended about 750 aliens whose immigration paperwork was improper and whom they suspected of having connections to the plane hijackers. There were many complaints raised by civil rights activists about the legal irregularities of this detention, and, in 2003, the Justice Department's Office of the Inspector General released a report that was, in places, highly critical of the government's methods. What seemed to some as a prudent roundup of people who had broken immigration regulations and were potential terrorists struck others as a cynical disregard for the rule of law made easier because the victims were "only" aliens.

The following chapters take a more detailed look at four central debates: the twin controversies of illegal and legal immigration, the question of English as an official language, and the issues of building physical barriers on the southern border.

◀||||POINT

# The United States Should Crack Down Harder on Illegal Immigrants

The Border Patrol agents found five-year-old Karen Tepas wandering through the desert in 100-degree heat, lost and crying for her mommy. The girl, streaked with dust and tears, had lost contact with her mother, who was seven months pregnant at the time, some miles back. The pair was part of a group being led by a *coyote*—a slang term for an immigrant smuggler—through the harsh borderlands along the U.S.-Mexico frontier, hoping to slip past the U.S. Immigration and Customs officials who patrol this barren territory. Karen did not get to stay in the United States, but nonetheless, she was one of the lucky ones. On average, every day one illegal immigrant dies trying to cross from the Mexican state of Sonora to Arizona during the hot summer months. The numbers are growing.[1]

Karen Tepas's case was, according to the Border Patrol, a common example of illegal immigration: She was accompanied

29

by one of her parents. Disturbing though her story may be, however, there is an even more ominous trend developing in the Sonora-Arizona frontier. Increasingly, U.S. and Mexican law enforcement agents are encountering children who are being smuggled overland by *coyotes* without any parent or guardian present. In 2007, the Office of Refugee Resettlement cared for 1,000 to 1,700 unaccompanied minors each month who were in their custody. These represent only the tip of the iceberg: No one has any idea how many children were successfully couriered into the United States in this way.[2]

The reason for the new smuggling tactic is simple: Parents who illegally immigrate to America have discovered that they have less chance of being detected if they enter alone and send for their children later. As one father put it, "We saw other people, our neighbors, hiring *coyotes* for their children. So we thought, why not us? We want the same things." The risks they take with their children are very real. "[*Coyotes*] are not Robin Hoods who are interested in helping families," says Joseph Greene, deputy assistant director for smuggling and public safety at United States Immigration and Customs Enforcement. "They are cold-blooded capitalists. The smugglers have seen children as the next important exploitable population." *Coyotes* often take few or no safety precautions, and there have been cases of children almost suffocating in the trunks of cars. Kidnapping, extortion, and abuse are constant hazards. Yet mothers and fathers continue to finance this deadly trade, immediately sending their children out into the desert again after detention by the Customs authorities. "We try to protect the children the best that we can. But the parents deceive us," said Bilha Villalobos, director of a Casa YMCA that looks after children caught with coyotes. Given that a first-time offender is likely to get a lesser punishment for smuggling a child than he would a sack of marijuana, it is no wonder that the supply of available couriers is as rich as ever.[3]

## America is facing an unprecedented wave of illegal immigration.

Whenever the subject of illegal immigration comes up, people immediately think of the problems along the southern U.S. border, and that long and inadequately patrolled frontier certainly is an important conduit for unregistered aliens attempting to enter the United States. Illegal immigrants come to America from every part of the world, however, and for all sorts of reasons. Visitors from Western Europe decide to supplement their tourist dollars in the United States by a little discreet work in the bars and restaurants of popular shore towns. Foreign students and employees overstay their nonimmigrant visas either because they don't wish to return to their home countries or because they hope to find a legitimate job in America. Agricultural laborers from Mexico do seasonal stints at American farms, vineyards, and orchards, returning south after the year's crop is harvested. Poverty-stricken workers from Africa and Asia serve as cheap undocumented manpower on construction sites, usually with the knowledge of the foreman. Hispanic domestic cleaners and nannies work for otherwise law-abiding families in exclusive neighborhoods—often with terrible pay and in exploitative conditions. The number of different scenarios is extremely varied.

Although illegal immigrants cannot be reduced to a simplistic caricature, it *is* possible to state with confidence that their numbers are increasing—perhaps drastically. In the Introduction, the figure of 11.3 million undocumented aliens now residing in the United States was given. That is the official government estimate from the Census Bureau, but it is quite possible that the real figure is much higher. The Federation for American Immigration Reform (FAIR) has argued that there may even be up to 13 million.[4] The numbers are growing rapidly: According to the Migration Policy Institute, it is estimated that, during the 1990s, the count increased by an annual average of 350,000, rising to 500,000 per year if you consider only the second half of the decade. By 2000, California had at least 2.2 million illegal immigrants, Texas had 1 million, and there were 1.3 million in New York, Illinois, and Florida combined. States that historically have had few undocumented aliens have seen an explosion in their numbers recently: Between 1990 and 2000, the number of

## The "Typical Illegal Alien"

One way to get a sense of what the illegal alien population is like is to look at the illegal aliens who were given amnesty in the late 1980s (under the Immigration Reform and Control Act of 1986). This group of almost three million illegal aliens, all of whom had been in the United States since before 1982, was made into legal aliens and has since been surveyed by the federal government. The government study (INS Report on the Legalized Alien Population, M-375, March 1992) found that out of the amnestied illegal alien population:

94 percent had migrated for economic reasons.
55 percent lived in California.
70 percent were from Mexico.
13 percent were from Central America.
74 percent had never been apprehended.
15 percent spoke English.
80 percent used public health services.
49 percent had no health insurance.

Their median age was 32, with an average household of four, seven years education, an hourly wage of $5.45, an annual individual income of $8,982, and annual family income of $15,364.

Remember, at the time of this survey, many of the illegal aliens were well established, having lived in the United States for over ten years. Many less successful illegal aliens would have left the country. The above profile of amnestied illegal aliens represented the most successful people in the illegal alien population. A profile of the overall illegal alien population could be expected to be much worse.

Source: Federation for American Immigration Reform, *Distribution of the Illegal Alien Population*, http://www.fairus.org/site/PageServer?pagename=iic_immigrationissuecentersdfe9

illegal immigrants in Nebraska, Iowa, Tennessee, and Arkansas rose by 300 percent to 400 percent, and North Carolina had a whopping 692 percent increase. More than two-thirds of these people came from Mexico, and during the same time period the overall number of Mexicans unlawfully residing in the United States increased by 140 percent.[5]

The problem with all of these figures is, of course, that they are at most educated guesses. Nobody really knows for sure how many illegal aliens there are in the United States, exactly where all of them are coming from, or to what degree their numbers are changing. All we can cautiously suggest from the evidence is that the figure is high and it is rising.

## Its effects on the United States are damaging.

So what? That is the response of some to the news that illegal immigration is on the increase. Isn't it, they argue, essentially a victimless crime? Yes, defiance of the law is never something to be applauded, but is it really a priority in this time of other pressing national concerns to hunt down undocumented aliens—people who are not really doing any harm and may even (by taking on jobs that Americans won't) be doing some good? Unfortunately, the reality is much bleaker than that. Illegal immigration hurts America by depressing wages and fostering unemployment; by raising taxes; by increasing the burden on public services such as schools, hospitals, and prisons; and by jeopardizing national security. It is also bad for illegal immigrants themselves—something that is often overlooked.

The Federation for American Immigration Reform estimates that about 730,000 American workers are displaced from their jobs every year because of competition from undocumented aliens.[6] To take one specific example, consider Clark County, Nevada, where one in seven residents are believed to be illegal immigrants. About 51,000, or more than two-thirds, of all construction employees in the county are working illegally. This cheap reserve of labor makes it impossible for American citizens to compete at a living wage. House framer William Ellis complains, "I started out making $800 to $1,200 a week here for a 40-hour week. It got to where I was having to work seven days a week, 12 hours a day, just to make $600 a week. And that's just in the past three or four years. The wage has gone down that bad." Everyone fares badly in this situation, because not only are legitimate workers squeezed out of the job market, but also the illegal immigrants are exploited by the unscrupulous employers who hire them.[7]

The costs can mount drastically; it is estimated that the cost of illegal immigrants to the U.S. taxpayer is $45 billion annually. This is after subtracting the amount contributed by illegal workers to the tax base. The strain on the judicial system nationwide is astonishing: Almost one-fifth of the federal prison population comes from Mexico, Colombia, Cuba, or the Dominican Republic.[8] The burden of educating the children of illegal immigrants in American public schools is more than $28.6 billion per year. In Texas, which makes up $3.9 billion of this total, the money spent could be used to cover the $2.3 billion budget shortfall that is needed for textbooks and classroom resources in the state.[9] Or look at California, which has the biggest undocumented-alien problem in the United States. The immigration-reform group FAIR found in a 2004 study that illegal immigration cost California taxpayers $10.5 billion per year. Even factoring in the tax contributions of illegal immigrants, the state paid out more than $9 billion to educate, provide health care, and incarcerate illegal aliens. Educating illegal immigrants and their children costs the state $7.7 billion as fully 15 percent of the students in California K-12 schools are children of illegal aliens.[10] This is an alarming diversion of resources when government budgets are already hard pressed to sustain social programs for citizens and legal residents.

Aside from the material cost, there is a very real risk to national security. Steven Camarota of the Center for Immigration Studies has pointed out that illegal immigrants have "taken part in almost every major attack on American soil perpetrated by Islamic terrorists, including the first attack on the World Trade Center, the Millennium plot, the plot to bomb the New York subway, and the attacks of 9/11."[11] This is not to demonize undocumented aliens, the vast majority of whom present no terrorist threat. Still, it would be folly to ignore the fact that, for example, five of the al-Qaeda hijackers who took part in the World Trade Center and Pentagon attacks were able to overstay their short-term visas without any apparent fear of being detected or punished by the immigration authorities.

Illegal immigrants are as much the victims of the smuggling trade as anyone, and the human price they pay just adds to the misery of the problem. Americans were aghast to hear of the 19 Mexicans who suffocated in a sealed container at a truck stop near Victoria, Texas, in May 2003, after being abandoned by their "guides." These kinds of deaths, though usually on a smaller scale, are not uncommon along the U.S.-Mexico border. Even illegal immigrants who pass safely into the United States often endure virtual slave-labor conditions. This "victimless" crime's first victims are the very people taking part.

## The United States is soft on illegal immigration.

What makes the situation even worse is that, far from trying to deter the further spread of illegal immigration, many lawmakers and business leaders in the United States today seem to be actively condoning its existence—and, by extension, encouraging it. In some cases, this is because of sheer despair at the scale of the problem—an understandable, if misguided, attitude. In others, the motive has more to do with vote buying from special-interest groups that have electoral power, or, in the case of businesses, an appetite for the money that can be made from illegal immigrants. Whatever the reason, the United States has developed a reputation as a "soft touch." It is not difficult to understand why.

Illegal immigrants are not supposed to be able to work, receive Social Security or welfare benefits (with the exception of

emergency medical care), or enjoy the various privileges associated with citizenship or permanent residency status. In reality,
however, millions of undocumented aliens take advantage of all
of these benefits every day. By using cheap and easily available
forged identification cards, they can establish supposedly legal
identities in the United States. Indeed, in many cases, it is not
even necessary to use counterfeit documents.

The Mexican government has been aggressively lobbying
American businesses and public services to accept its *Matricula
Consular* IDs, even though these are used almost exclusively by
illegal immigrants—Mexicans who are in the United States legitimately have access to other documents, such as passports and green

## "Latinos Want a Tighter Border, Too"

I am a Mexican American. I have proudly served my country in two wars, and
there are millions more like me. We are proud that our country's immigration laws
are far more generous than those of Mexico or any other place in the developed
world. But we are also proud that we are a nation of laws, which means respect for
laws, including those we may not like. And illegal immigration is just that: illegal.
It is a crime. To condone, encourage, perpetuate or defend it is unconscionable. To
aid and abet it is equally illegal.

It is one thing to break a country's laws when fleeing from persecution or when
your life is threatened. It is a totally different matter to break the law and hope to
profit. It is one thing to petition your own government for fair treatment. It is quite
another to make demands on a foreign government and its taxpayers when you
have illegally rushed across its borders. And it is a horrible thing to start your life
as a would-be American as a criminal.

This has nothing to do with race. If Latinos are caught more often, it is because
they illegally cross the border more often.... What's interesting in this debate is
the opinion of other Latinos. Maria Enchautegui, who has conducted immigration
studies for the Urban Institute, acknowledges that "Hispanics are affected most by
immigration. Hispanics compete more with new immigrants than do white and
black Americans. They feel the negative effects more."

cards. In California, possession of a *Matricula Consular* allows a person to open a bank account, cash checks, and travel by air—almost everything one needs for day-to-day living. (The irony is that Mexican banks will not accept these cards!) During the 2003 gubernatorial recall race in that state, then-Governor Gray Davis introduced a law that would allow illegal aliens to obtain California driver's licenses—a move that his critics called blatant pandering to the large number of undocumented aliens who were fraudulently on the electoral register. Elsewhere, some politicians want to allow undocumented aliens to claim Social Security payouts.[12]

Part of the problem is that too many American firms acquiesce in serving or hiring illegal immigrants, either because they

*Dallas Morning News* columnist Richard Estrada says, "The rank and file Hispanics were far ahead of other Americans in viewing illegal immigrants as economic and even social threats...because the effects of immigration have manifested themselves first and foremost in Hispanic communities of long standing."

The respected magazine *Hispanic* says, "There is an ironic inconsistency in the U.S. Hispanic community. On the one hand, Hispanic Americans have become subjects of an anti-immigration backlash, while on the other, the majority opposes current levels of immigration. Up to 84% say there are already too many immigrants coming into the United States." *Hispanic*'s report was based on the Latino National Political Survey, which, the magazine said, is considered the most sweeping measure to date of Latino opinion on social and political topics."

...Illegal immigration has become a big business, with the local taxpayer bearing the costs. It provides a pressure valve for Mexico, so instead of caring for its own people, Mexico ships them north. Our paralyzed legislators don't fight, acting like deer transfixed in headlights. Our $2-an-hour "employers" welcome it; it's the next best thing to getting workers free. Drug abusers need it; the coyotes carry their mail.

And so it goes, on and on and on, like the Energizer Bunny.

Source: Jesse Laguna, "Latinos Want a Tighter Border, Too," *Los Angeles Times*, September 23, 1994.

want the business immigrants bring or because immigrants provide a cheap (and union-free) supply of labor. Even keystone American businesses have been implicated in this policy of looking the other way. In November 2003, the giant retailer Wal-Mart was placed under a federal grand jury investigation after it was discovered that some of the firms it subcontracts to clean its stores were employing aliens from Latin America and Eastern Europe.[13] According to a travel agent in the Czech Republic who admitted to arranging illegal placements for foreign workers in league with American companies, "Every second person who buys a plane ticket to the United States at my agency goes there to make money. I would say that the U.S. authorities turn a blind eye."[14]

Illegal immigrants know that the chances of being apprehended by U.S. immigration authorities are slim. Between 1990 and 2000, the INS managed to deport only 412,000 undocumented aliens—this during a period in which the total number of illegal immigrants was estimated to have increased by at least 5.5 million.[15] When the government *does* act, it often finds itself obstructed by local politicians and law enforcement agencies who have their own agendas. For example, in a 1998–1999 operation in the meat-packing plants of Nebraska, the INS audited the personnel records of all employees and successfully drove out the illegal immigrants working there—only to face the staunch opposition of a regional lobby that succeeded in closing the operation and forcing its leader to take early retirement.[16] With these kinds of conditions, it is no wonder that federal immigration officials have effectively given up trying to tackle the undocumented-alien problem. It is equally unsurprising that the illegal immigrants themselves have contempt for the law.

### Amnesty is not the answer.
One suggestion that has been proposed to "solve" the illegal-immigration problem is amnesty—allowing certain classes of undocumented aliens to become permanent residents of the

United States, usually on the basis of the work that they do or the number of years they have lived illicitly in the country. In 1986, the Immigration Reform and Control Act (IRCA) amnestied 2.8 million illegal aliens who had been residing in the United States for four or more years or who worked in the agricultural sector. Throughout his presidency, the former Mexican president, Vicente Fox pressed the administration of President George W. Bush to develop an amnesty program that would cover some of the millions of illegal immigrants who arrived in the United States during the 1990s, many of whom originally came from Mexico. Similar to his predecessor, Mexico's current president, Felipe Calderón, seems equally interested in immigration reform, including some types of amnesty. Amnesty doesn't solve the basic problem at the heart of illegal immigration, however; in many ways it makes it worse.

Amnesty *appears* to reduce the problem of undocumented aliens by making them legal residents—in other words, by changing their administrative status at the stroke of a pen. The people involved, though, are unchanged by this sleight-of-hand, and illegal immigrants are on average far less educated and trained than foreign-born residents who receive immigrant visas the conventional way. This is the least desirable type of immigrant for a high-wage, high-skill economy. Why should we invite large numbers of them to live in the United States simply because they broke the law in the first place? This seems no less absurd than rewarding muggers with cash payments or presenting gifts to thieves. The problem does not disappear because of a change of labels: A Center for Immigration Studies analysis suggests that the IRCA amnesty caused an overall *increase* in the number of undocumented aliens, because of family members joining their newly legalized relatives.[17]

Amnesty is more than just an abandonment of the government's responsibility to uphold the law; it is also an active affront to law-abiding citizens and a powerful incentive to those who might be thinking of becoming undocumented aliens. Its contempt for legal immigrants should not be ignored. Is it fair that people who have patiently waited their turn and gone through the proper immigration procedures, sometimes taking many years, should be passed over in favor of those who either could not or would not? There is something perverse about a policy that favors people who are less suited to living in the United States and have done the least to deserve it.

## Summary

Illegal aliens are not monsters. They are ordinary people trying to make hard decisions in difficult circumstances. Even when they break the law, they deserve to be treated with decency and dignity in the spirit of the U.S. Constitution and the Bill of Rights. Nevertheless, the United States is not obliged to accept them simply because they want to come here. It is really our fault, not theirs, that illegal immigration has become the massive problem it is today. If our laws had not become so riddled with loopholes, our immigration officials so reluctant to efficiently track and deport undocumented residents, and our businesses so willing to hire them with no questions asked, illegal immigration would be a much less acute dilemma. The solution—tough, effective laws, properly implemented, with self-restraint on the part of employers—lies with *us*, not with them.

# The Key to Stopping Illegal Immigration Is to Reform the Law, Not to Punish People

In November 1999, a six-year-old boy clinging to a rubber tube arrived in the United States of America and, for a few dramatic months, turned the country's political world upside-down. His name was Elián Gonzalez, and he was the only survivor of a group of 11 Cuban refugees whose boat sank as they were trying to make it to the Florida coast to claim political asylum. Elián's mother died in the voyage, but it turned out that the boy's father, who was not involved in the escape, was alive and well back in Cuba. After the news broke that his child had been rescued and taken to the United States, he petitioned the American government to have the boy returned. Then the storm really broke. Elián's relatives in Miami made a passionate bid that the child not be sent back to Fidel Castro's dictatorial regime and that he should be allowed to live with them instead—regardless of the fact that, in cases such as these, the surviving parent usually has the absolute right to custody of the child.

Elián became a cultural icon, his image adorning newspaper front pages, magazine covers, and TV screens across the nation. ABC journalist Diane Sawyer obtained an exclusive interview with Elián, which was sympathetic to the arguments of the Miami relatives: "How can the U.S. government enforce the law without hurting a little boy?" she asked.[1] Washington politicians got involved, with a bipartisan Senate bill being introduced to grant Elián permanent residency status. Other lawmakers lambasted the Justice Department for its plans to return Elián to Cuba. There was even a suggestion that the boy be made an honorary U.S. citizen in order to keep him in the country; this procedure is normally used only to pay tribute to distinguished foreign personalities such as Winston Churchill and Mother Teresa. Eventually, immigration officials took custody of Elián in a controversial dawn raid on the relatives' home in April 2000, and he was promptly dispatched back to Cuba. Since then, he has apparently adjusted back to life with his father, and the saga that once enthralled America has largely disappeared from popular memory.

Can we learn anything about our own country from the Elián Gonzalez case? Certainly there is one revealing element to the story: our completely inconsistent attitude toward illegal immigrants. Elián was an undocumented alien who arrived in the United States without authorization, just like millions of other men, women, and children. He was one of "them," the dreaded foreign hordes that politicians regularly tell us threaten our homes, our jobs, and our way of life. If he had been just another anonymous, less newsworthy statistic, his case would not have been given a second thought and those statesmen and reporters who scrambled to defend him would not have shown the slightest interest in his fate.

Instead, he was an attractive, smiling, human being, "a beautiful young child who arrived here in a kind of a mythic condition, washed up on our shore on Thanksgiving Day in a vain attempt by his mother to escape tyranny—a rather classical American story."[2] His case made for exciting and emotional news. Moreover, he was a Cuban—and the Cuban-American constituency in Florida was a vital voting bloc in the 2000 presidential election. "It's a good bet that had this been, say, a Haitian child, the law-and-order folks would have raided the place weeks ago, and none of us would have even known it was happening," Judy Mann pointed out in the *Washington Post* shortly after Elián was removed from his relatives' home.[3] Illegal immigrants are the enemy, it seems—except when they come in photogenic packages and make for useful political slogans.

## The United States needs illegal immigrants more than it is willing to admit.

It is no wonder, really, that America's attitude toward illegal immigration is schizophrenic. The U.S. economic and legal system draws undocumented aliens in at the same time that it pushes them away. As stated in the Introduction, it is extremely difficult to gain lawful entry to the United States on employment grounds without exceptional education and skills. Yet, as Nolo Martinez pointed out in a 2003 commentary,

> It was the demand for unskilled or semi-skilled workers employed in all sectors of the U.S. economy that increased at enormous rates in the 1990s and will continue to rise to new levels during the next 10 years. These workers include restaurant workers, retail clerks, construction workers, manufacturing line workers, hotel service workers, landscape workers and health care aides.[4]

Such jobs—unglamorous, physically grueling, monotonous, yet vital—are unattractive to American citizens, but they are perfect for immigrants who are willing to do them in order to become established in the United States and who will work for relatively low wages. Yet employers cannot hire immigrants legally because of visa restrictions. The inevitable result is the tacit recruitment of undocumented aliens, often from Mexico or elsewhere in Latin America.

It is not just businesses that turn a blind eye to this practice; in effect, we all do. As much as we might want to complain about "illegals," we enjoy considerable monetary benefits because of their presence. Large sectors of the American economy, such as agriculture, simply would not work without the hiring of undocumented aliens. Or, rather, they might work—but only if we were willing to pay, say, $10 for a head of lettuce or a bag of tomatoes. Even economics researcher Kruti Dholakia, who believes that immigration laws should be tightened, admits, "A lower amount of illegal immigrants could also mean a higher wage rate prevailing in the economy[,] especially for low-skilled or unskilled jobs, which would lead to high cost and lack of competitiveness for U.S. goods using those kinds of labor."[5] This does not mean that we should do nothing about illegal immigration, but we need to admit that the United States has a complex, love-hate relationship with its "uninvited guests."

Indeed, illegal immigration plays such an important role in the economy that its net effects are highly *positive*. One estimate suggests that, in California, which is home to about half of all the illegal immigrants in the United States, the input of these undocumented workers to the state economy is about $63 billion annually— approximately 7 percent of California's overall economic activity, or about $45,000 per immigrant per year. Because few illegal immigrants can take advantage of health, welfare, or other social services, for fear of detection by the authorities, their demands on the public purse are very small compared with their contributions. "Instead of the state and nation subsidizing immigrants," activist Tim Wise concludes, "it is more accurate to say that immigrants subsidize the economy and the companies for which they work by performing low-wage labor that is worth at least four times more, on average, than what they earn from income and welfare combined."[6]

## The real victims are undocumented aliens themselves.

As we can see, the "damage" inflicted by illegal immigrants on America is debatable. The suffering undocumented aliens endure while resident in the United States is no myth, however. Having been attracted to this country by the lure of employment, illegal immigrants find themselves routinely exploited, abused, and with little recourse to, or protection from, the law.

Hilda Rosa Dos Santos's story is an example of the failures of the current system. Dos Santos came to the United States in 1979, accompanying an affluent Brazilian family that intended her to work for them as a domestic employee. In fact, she was more slave than servant: Dos Santos was forced to sleep in a small window-less room, was given little to eat, and was routinely attacked by the wife of her employer, who poured hot soup on her and yanked out her hair. Because the illiterate Portuguese-speaking woman's visa had expired a couple of years after her arrival in the United States, her abusers were able to intimidate her into remaining silent about her ordeal. For 20 years, they kept Dos Santos in these appalling conditions, until she was finally rescued by sympathetic neighbors who were worried about her medical state—she had a stomach tumor the size of a soccer ball for which, needless to say, her employers had refused to provide medical attention. The courts finally did some justice on Dos Santos's behalf, sentencing her jailer to more than six years in prison and awarding her $110,000 in restitution.[7] Her traumatic experience is by no means unique. Thousands more undocumented aliens live in similar conditions, abandoned by a society that sees them only as criminals and not as victims of an exploitative economic system.

Even more benign employers who would never dream of physically abusing undocumented aliens often exploit the aliens' ambivalent legal status by paying them miserly wages and refusing to provide the Social Security contributions the law demands. Perhaps the most notorious example of this was the "Nannygate" scandal in early 1993, when it was revealed that President Bill

Clinton's nominee for attorney general, Zoë Baird, had employed two illegal Peruvian immigrants to look after her young child. What made Baird's behavior even more outrageous in the public

# THE LETTER OF THE LAW

## Extracts from California's 1994 Proposition 187

SECTION 1. Findings and Declaration.

The People of California find and declare as follows:

That they have suffered and are suffering economic hardship caused by the presence of illegal aliens in this state.

That they have suffered and are suffering personal injury and damage caused by the criminal conduct of illegal aliens in this state.

That they have a right to the protection of their government from any person or persons entering this country unlawfully.

Therefore, the People of California declare their intention to provide for cooperation between their agencies of state and local government with the federal government, and to establish a system of required notification by and between such agencies to prevent illegal aliens in the United States from receiving benefits or public services in the State of California.

SECTION 5. Exclusion of Illegal Aliens from Public Social Services.

(a) In order to carry out the intention of the People of California that only citizens of the United States and aliens lawfully admitted to the United States may receive the benefits of public social services and to ensure that all persons employed in the providing of those services shall diligently protect public funds from misuse, the provisions of this section are adopted.

(b) A person shall not receive any public social services to which he or she may be otherwise entitled until the legal status of that person has been verified as one of the following:

(1) A citizen of the United States. (2) An alien lawfully admitted as a permanent resident. (3) An alien lawfully admitted for a temporary period of time.

SECTION 6. Exclusion of Illegal Aliens from Publicly Funded Health Care.

(a) In order to carry out the intention of the People of California that, excepting emergency medical care as required by federal law, only citizens of the United

eye was that while she was earning $500,000 per year as a lawyer, she had paid her nannies just $500 a week and had ignored Social Security requirements. It was estimated at the time that about

States and aliens lawfully admitted to the United States may receive the benefits of publicly-funded health care, and to ensure that all persons employed in the providing of those services shall diligently protect public funds from misuse, the provisions of this section are adopted.

(b) A person shall not receive any health care services from a publicly-funded health care facility, to which he or she is otherwise entitled until the legal status of that person has been verified as one of the following:

(1) A citizen of the United States. (2) An alien lawfully admitted as a permanent resident. (3) An alien lawfully admitted for a temporary period of time.

SECTION 7. Exclusion of Illegal Aliens from Public Elementary and Secondary Schools.

(a) No public elementary or secondary school shall admit, or permit the attendance of, any child who is not a citizen of the United States, an alien lawfully admitted as a permanent resident, or a person who is otherwise authorized under federal law to be present in the United States.

(b) Commencing January 1, 1995, each school district shall verify the legal status of each child enrolling in the school district for the first time in order to ensure the enrollment or attendance only of citizens, aliens lawfully admitted as permanent residents, or persons who are otherwise authorized to be present in the United States.

(c) By January 1, 1996, each school district shall have verified the legal status of each child already enrolled and in attendance in the school district in order to ensure the enrollment or attendance only of citizens, aliens lawfully admitted as permanent residents, or persons who are otherwise authorized under federal law to be present in the United States.

Source: The full text of this document can be found at http://www.americanpatrol.com/ REFERENCE/prop187text.html

2 million families were employing domestic workers, many of them illegally, and only one-quarter of these were paying taxes.[8]

## Attempts to toughen laws are often counterproductive.

Advocates of tougher policies for illegal immigration argue that the best way to prevent this abuse and exploitation is to make it more difficult and more unappealing for undocumented aliens to enter the United States in the first place. The problem with this approach is that attempts to stiffen the rules often make the situation worse rather than better.

In November 1994, California voters approved a popular ballot measure known as Proposition 187, which would have prevented illegal aliens from receiving welfare benefits, barred undocumented children from California schools, and required state agencies to pass along information about known illegal aliens to law enforcement officials. Because of legal wrangles, Proposition 187 lingered in legal limbo for five years until, in 1999, a settlement between the state government and civil rights organizations effectively killed it off.

What would have been the proposition's effect if it had ever been implemented? Its supporters argued that it would choke off illegal immigration into the state and reduce California's high budget deficits. These claims are questionable. Illegal immigration already involves great risk and sacrifice on the part of those involved; people who have literally risked their lives to come to the United States are unlikely to be dissuaded simply by the threat of a loss of a few welfare opportunities. Is it really a good idea to deprive residents of medical and education benefits when the result may be public health fears—infectious disease is no respecter of citizenship—and juvenile delinquency? "Prop 187 will not solve anything because it is unrealistic about the sources of the state's problems and the ability of the government to control people's action," Jeff Lustig and Dick Walker of the Berkeley, California-based Campus Coalition for Human Rights and Social Justice argued in 1995. "It will not stop so-called 'illegal' immigration. . . . [n]or will it revive the economy, free up jobs for the unemployed or bring us back together as a people. It would move us instead toward a caste-divided, fortress state."[9] Much the same could be said about the government's recent attempts to tighten border restrictions along the U.S.-Mexico frontier. Despite much fanfare and talk of the need for added security in the wake of the 9/11 attacks and the threat of terrorism, the crackdown has had little practical effect on homeland defense *or* the problem of illegal immigration: "The tightening net of Border Patrol and Immigration agents has slowed trade, snarled traffic and cost American taxpayers millions, perhaps billions, of dollars," stated the Associated Press, "while hundreds of migrants have died trying to evade the growing army of border authorities"[10] Such crude attempts to solve as big a problem as illegal immigration typically backfire.

## Amnesty would reduce many of the problems of illegal immigration.

What *should* be done about undocumented aliens? Everyone more or less agrees that the present situation is undesirable. The question is not whether we can maintain the status quo but how we should reform the law to provide the best outcome for immigrants *and* Americans as a whole. The best solution, in the eyes of many activists, would be a comprehensive amnesty—a legalization of those undocumented immigrants currently living a shadowy life within the United States. As one St. Louis newspaper put it in 2003:

> There is in America a downtrodden group of 7 million people to whom the blessings of freedom and liberty do not apply. They dare not call the police when they're robbed. Their bosses can cheat them, and they'll never complain. They are, of course, illegal immigrants. . . . . They broke American law to get here, which can't be condoned. But they came for the same

## Linda Chavez-Thompson on Exploited Workers in America Today

Growing up in western Texas as the daughter of cotton sharecroppers, I spent my summers weeding cotton, five days a week, 10 hours a day, in 95-degree heat. As grueling as this workload was, others had it even worse.

For foreign workers toiling as "guest workers" (or "braceros") alongside us in the cotton fields, the five-day work week was an impossible luxury. They were often stiffed on wages, and health care was simply non-existent. Viewing them as units of production, employers worked them to their limit, knowing that the following season a fresh unsuspecting batch would arrive.

The horrific abuses suffered by workers in programs such as the bracero program are well documented and indisputable. And although most people like to think of bracero programs as a phenomenon of the past, the reality is that their legacy of exploitation and abuse continues to thrive in contemporary American society through modern guest worker programs such as the H2-A and H2-B.

Like undocumented workers, "guest workers" in this country face enormous obstacles in enforcing their labor rights.

The H-2 guest worker programs bring in agricultural and other seasonal workers to pick crops, do construction and work in the seafood industry, among other jobs. Workers typically borrow large amounts of money to pay travel expenses, fees and even bribes to recruiters. That means that before they even begin to work, they are indebted.

According to a new study published by the Southern Poverty Law Center, it is not unusual for a Guatemalan worker to pay more than $2,500 in fees to obtain a seasonal guest worker position, about a year's worth of income in Guatemala. And Thai workers have been known to pay as much as $10,000 for the chance to harvest crops in the orchards of the Pacific Northwest. Interest rates on the loans are sometimes as high as 20% a month. Homes and vehicles are required collateral.

Handcuffed by their debt and bound to employers who can send them home on a whim, the "guests" are forced to remain and work for employers even when their pay and working conditions are second-rate, hazardous or abusive. Hungry children inevitably trump protest. Technically, these programs include some legal protections, but in reality, those protections exist mostly on paper. Government enforcement is almost nonexistent. Private attorneys refuse to take cases, and language barriers make it virtually impossible for workers to speak out.

Undocumented immigrants face similar obstacles at work. Because they are under the constant threat of deportation, they cannot effectively assert their rights at the workplace, and employers routinely take advantage of them.

The result is that both guest workers and undocumented workers end up working the most dangerous and most exploitative jobs in our country.

It's getting worse, not better. Among foreign-born workers, workplace fatalities increased by an alarming 46% between 1992 and 2002. Since 1992, fatalities among Hispanic workers have increased by 65%.

When immigrant workers try to correct such injustices by forming unions, they are cruelly harassed, intimidated and even terminated for their actions. When all else fails to break a union drive, employers simply call in the immigration authorities and everyone gets deported for standing up for basic rights.

For years, the AFL-CIO has campaigned for an end to the exploitation and abuse of immigrant workers who are here working hard and contributing to our economy. The best way to guarantee the rights and wages of all workers in this country is to give every immigrant the opportunity to become a citizen, with all the rights and duties that entails.

The exploitation of immigrant workers hurts us all. When standards are driven down for some workers, they are driven down for all workers. For this same reason, guest worker programs must be squarely rejected. Because workers in these programs are always dependent on their host employers for both their livelihoods and legal status, these programs create a disenfranchised underclass of workers.

History, economics and common sense dictate that exploitation of workers will continue as long as it makes economic sense for employers to do so. We must step outside of the status quo and revise the current immigration law in a way that guarantees full labor rights for future foreign workers and reflects real labor market conditions by restructuring the current permanent employment visa category. That is, future foreign workers should be welcomed as permanent residents with full rights at the onset—not as disposable "guests." This is the only way to guarantee that foreign workers enjoy the same rights and protections as all other U.S. workers, including the freedom to form unions and bargain for a better life.

As a nation that prides itself on fair treatment and equality, how can we possibly settle for anything less?

Source: Linda Chavez-Thompson, "It's Time To End Worker Exploitation," Forbes.com, June 6, 2007. http://www.forbes.com/2007/06/05/labor-immigrants-workers-oped-cx_lct_0606labor.html

reason that most of our own ancestors did—for a better life for their families. And they're not going away.

Years of trying to handle illegal immigration by punitive laws and fear of prosecution have gotten us nowhere. All they have produced is a twilight culture in which undocumented aliens live in a permanently criminalized state, often reduced to lawbreaking in order to sustain themselves, and without the ability to assimilate into the American mainstream as previous generations of immigrants did.

If we were to start fresh and legalize all illegal aliens living in the United States, we could end the cycle of exploitation that has corrupted the world of low-paying domestic and manual labor in which illegal immigrants currently predominate. Of course, an immediate objection to amnesty is that it would reward previous criminal behavior and encourage many more undocumented aliens to try to enter the country. No one wants to minimize the necessity of keeping within the law, but the United States has long recognized the importance of a fresh start for offenders, which is why we have a parole and rehabilitation system. Amnesty would give millions of people who have lived in the United States for years the chance of a fresh start. As the *St. Louis Post-Dispatch* observed: "This nation was founded on the principle of human equality. It offends that principle to keep people living in the shadows, working in sweatshops and in fear."[11] As for the future, amnesty will really work only in conjunction with a new and better policy toward immigration as a whole, one that provides the labor force American companies demand while reducing the need to enter the country unlawfully. One idea that has recently been proposed is an expanded "guest worker" program, which is discussed in the conclusion to this book.

## Summary

It is not easy to find anyone in American public life who will say a good word for illegal immigrants. They have become the convenient scapegoats for all kinds of contentious issues—unemployment, welfare, crime, national security. How easy it is for politicians to blame our failings on those who cannot vote! How much harder, and braver, it would be to admit that undocumented aliens are living here by the invitation of our fellow Americans—established companies, agricultural concerns, and even high-flying professionals who want cheap child care and domestic help with no questions asked. We *need* illegal immigrants; our economy demands their presence. The fact that they must break the law to come here is a fault of *our* immigration policy. The people who ultimately pay the price for this flawed system are the immigrants themselves. Let us stop the cheap attacks on the most downtrodden members of our community and bring them into the national fold rather than treating them as convenient but ultimately disposable pariahs.

# The United States Should Construct Physical Barriers on the Southern Border to Stem the Tide of Illegal Immigration

I n April 2005, nearly 900 retired school teachers, CEOs, and other volunteers spent time camped out in the desert on the Mexican-U.S. border. Not merely adventure campers or extreme vacation types, the group came to this dusty part of Arizona with a common purpose—to patrol and eventually highlight the porous nature of the nearly 2,000-mile-long border with Mexico. This common purpose was inspired by what they viewed as a lack of action by the government to secure the border. Pickup trucks, RVs, and tents dotted the border as volunteers, often seated in lawn chairs and equipped with binoculars, scanned the horizon for signs of illegal immigrants trying to make it into the United States. While some were armed with guns, all were outfitted with cell phones to contact Border Patrol agents when they saw activity. By the end of the month, 330 illegal immigrants had been apprehended because of calls by the self-proclaimed "Minutemen volunteers."[1]

The citizen border-security idea behind the Minutemen movement can also be seen in the Border Fence Project (BFP). Organizers of the BFP also believe that inaction by the government means private citizens need to secure the border on their own. The BFP coordinates volunteers who pay for and erect fencing along the southern border of the United States. As of mid-2008, they have already constructed more than four miles of fencing. From this modest start, the BFP plans to extend a fence across all 1,950 miles of the southern border, at a cost projection of $50 million.[2]

So why are these groups, and others like them, concerned about physically securing the borders, especially the southern border with Mexico? These groups, and their many supporters, recognize that border security is crucial for any nation, particularly in these times of economic and security unease. Without a strong, physical border that effectively controls the flow of people into and out of a nation, that nation cannot maintain economic and strategic safety.

## Physical borders are needed to maintain national security.

Every nation must secure its borders in order to maintain its national sovereignty. As congressman and wild-card presidential candidate Ron Paul explains, "[w]e must secure our borders now. A nation without secure borders is no nation at all. It makes no sense to fight terrorists abroad when our own front door is left unlocked."[3] The fact that sovereign nations have a right, even a duty, to protect and control their borders is widely recognized in international law.[4] The U.S. Constitution even empowers Congress to raise a militia to repel invasions.[5] It is not hard to argue that the 11 million to 13 million illegal immigrants in this country are an invasion to which Congress has a duty to respond.[6]

Even if the United States were not facing an uncertain security situation internationally, the government would have a duty to protect our borders from being overrun by people whom we could not document or regulate. September 11, 2001, however, demonstrated that the United States is being targeted by people intent on doing harm to the country and its people.[7] Even years after the terrorist attacks, U.S. intelligence reports that narco-terrorists, drug gangs, and other international terrorist groups are preparing and have attacked the U.S. homeland by crossing the U.S.-Mexico border. Controlling who crosses into the United States is one commonsense way of limiting these kinds of future attacks.[8]

## A fence will help stem illegal activity in border regions.

Tied to both security and economic concerns is the illegal trade that occurs along the U.S.-Mexico border. Drug runners and human traffickers frequently use this rather porous border to trade in their illicit cargos. According to the Drug Enforcement Administration (DEA), drug trafficking organizations (DTOs) rely heavily on the southwestern border:

> The Southwest Border Region is the most significant national-level storage, transportation, and transshipment area for illicit drug shipments that are destined for drug markets throughout the United States. The region is the principal arrival zone for most drugs smuggled into the United States; more illicit drugs are seized along the Southwest Border than in any other arrival zone.

The DEA is also concerned with human smuggling, especially by human traffickers known as *coyotes*:

> The Southwest Border Region is the principal entry point for undocumented aliens from Mexico, Central America, and South America. Undocumented aliens from special-interest countries such as Afghanistan, Iran, Iraq, and Pakistan also illegally enter the United States through the region. Mexican

DTOs collect fees from alien smuggling organizations for the use of specific smuggling routes. Among those individuals illegally crossing the border are criminal aliens and gang members who pose public safety concerns for communities throughout the country. In addition, hundreds of undocumented aliens from special-interest countries illegally cross the U.S.-Mexico border annually. Available reporting indicates that some alien smuggling organizations and Mexican DTOs specialize in smuggling special-interest aliens into the United States.

Along with the smuggling of various contraband come the waves of violence associated with these kinds of illegal activities. Arizona in particular has seen a wave of DTO violence as rival gangs battle for smuggling routes and clientele.[9]

## A barrier on the border is a practical solution.

So what can be done to stop this wave of illegal immigration into the United States? One proposal that is supported by many Americans is to secure the border physically with a fence or other barrier.[10] The idea is nothing new. Sections of the U.S.-Mexico border have long had fencing and other barriers, especially near official crossing areas. After the 9/11 attacks, however, a movement to secure the entire southern border began in earnest. In response, Congress passed a bill funding 700 miles of fencing for the southern border, with an eventual goal of protecting the entire 2,000-mile border with fencing and electronic surveillance, or "smart fencing." On October 26, 2006, President Bush signed the bill into law.[11]

Since the passage of that bill, about 300 miles of fence have been put into place and results are evident, despite some resistance and slowdowns. In San Diego, stadium lighting, surveillance cameras, double fences, and electronic detection equipment now cover five miles of the border—the same stretch of land where masses of people illegally entered the United States in the early to mid-1990s.

The San Diego sector's chief, Michael Fisher, noted, "Over the years the San Diego sector has been able to incrementally gain operational control of this area." The proof of the success of the barrier in this area can be seen in the drop in numbers of apprehensions in this area. In the 1990s, apprehensions along the San Diego sector averaged 600,000 per year, while in 2007 only 153,000 people were apprehended attempting to cross the border illegally. The wall has not stopped all illegal entry, but it has made a difference and given law enforcement some sense of control over this section of the border.[12]

Barriers of this kind are even more effective when combined with other tactics that Border Patrol and immigration officials are using to stanch the flow at the border. Homeland Security Secretary Michael Chertoff testified before Congress that immigration agencies are modifying their response to illegal aliens captured at the U.S.-Mexico border. Historically U.S. policy was known as "catch and release," where apprehended aliens were fingerprinted and then released back to Mexico. Under Operation Streamline, the new policy has been to "catch and return," whereby everyone caught illegally entering the country is arrested and charged with at least misdemeanor immigration charges, detained, and eventually returned to Mexico. The benefit of "catch and return" policies is that people who illegally enter the United States will have a criminal record that will limit their ability to enter the country legally in the future. Federal officials such as Chertoff believe this disincentive contributed to the nearly 20 percent drop in apprehensions in 2007.[13]

In 2006, a joint U.S.-Mexico drug bust found a 2,400-foot-long tunnel stretching from Tijuana, Mexico, to Otay Mesa, California. In the tunnel, agents seized about two tons of marijuana that was being smuggled in. The tunnel was incredibly work intensive. These kinds of discoveries show that criminals are having to expend far more resources and energy to conduct their enterprises. When questioned about the discovery of the tunnel, Bill Morrow, a California state senator, said, "this demonstrates that the border fence is a success. We're driving them underground. It makes it easier to find them, in that respect."[14]

## Adequate options are available for high- and low-traffic areas.

The Department of Human Services has described the plans for the U.S. border fence to include physical fencing, technological fencing, and natural barriers as means of stopping illegal immigration across the border. The physical fencing will include corrugated steel, chain link, and concrete walls in places where illegal immigrants could easily blend in with large population areas and go undetected. In more remote areas where vehicles would have to be used, the CBP would use a range of fencing, including:

- vehicle bollards similar to those found around federal buildings

- "post on rail" steel set in concrete with a mesh option

- steel picket-style fence set in concrete

- concrete jersey walls with steel mesh

- a "Normandy" vehicle fence consisting of steel beams

According to the Department of Homeland Security Web site, technological fencing would include, "[i]n remote areas along the border, tower-based integrated cameras and sensors, ground-based radar, mobile surveillance systems, and an unmanned aerial system along with traditional border patrols. These tools are part of CBP's technology solution." Finally, geographic barriers such as mountains, rivers, and other difficult-to-pass natural occurrences would be integrated into the border scheme. Ultimately, the entire 2,000-mile border between the United States and Mexico is slated to be monitored and/or barrier controlled by 2010.[15]

## Criticisms of the border fence are unfounded.

Critics of the wall argue that the fence is ineffective, too costly, and damaging to the environment. The system in San Diego is evidence against the first two critiques, and Congress and the courts have dealt with the latter. It is true that the fence has not stopped every person wanting to enter the United States undetected. Border Patrol agents continue to discover inventive ways individuals have developed to cross the border, from tunnel systems to converted freight systems to jumping over the fences. No system will keep out every person attempting to break U.S. law and enter the United States illegally. It is still worth the effort to reduce lawless activity where possible. To follow the logic of those who would not put up the fence because not every person would be caught, it would follow that police should not hand out traffic tickets or arrest burglars, because they cannot catch every single offender. Surely a nation of laws does not have to be perfect in its work to police itself effectively.

As to the assertion that the wall is too costly, one has only to look at the overall cost of illegal immigration to realize the futility of this argument. It is true that the fence project is more expensive than originally projected. With cost overruns, the fence is costing approximately $3 million per mile. For the 670 miles of border that are scheduled to be fenced, the price tag is now $1.2 billion. When factoring in the cost of upkeep and repair for the fence, the total cost is $50 billion. Undoubtedly this is a huge amount of money, but as pointed out earlier, the cost of aliens living in this country illegally is estimated to be $45 billion *a year*. Even if initial costs are more than expected, the fence should pay for itself over the next few years in the number of illegal aliens it deters.[16]

Finally, much has been made of the environmental impact of the border wall. Environmental groups claim that the wall will affect coastal areas when it nears the ocean, and that migratory animals such as the jaguar and pronghorns travel through the desert areas.[17] In the face of threatened lawsuits by environmental groups and interference from various state and federal agencies, Congress provided the Department of Homeland Security the power to override the rules of various environmental agencies if they interfered with the building of the border fence. Chertoff used this power to overrule many federal rules requiring environmental impact studies and other time-intensive procedures. Chertoff cited national security as the primary motivation for exercising this power, but also mentioned the environmental damage being done by illegal immigrants in trampling sensitive vegetation, trails, and garbage being discarded along the border. Chertoff's decision has been upheld by courts, and seems to make clear that the border wall is going to go up as planned.[18]

## Summary

The southwestern border region of the United States has long been an entry point for illegal immigrants and criminals who traffic their contraband into the United States. Such porous borders are dangerous to the security and safety of the citizens of the United States, as well as to those who try to cross it illegally. It is the government's duty to physically secure this border and to stop the smuggled goods as well as the violence that comes with it.

Building a barrier on the border is the best solution to solving this problem. While it is not a perfect barrier to illicit activity on the border, its presence is an integral part of a larger program to secure the border. While some may criticize physical barriers at the border, they are the most effective, most cost efficient and most environmentally friendly method available for border security at this time.

# Physical Barriers on the U.S. Southern Border Will Not Solve Illegal Immigration Problems

In November 1961, President John F. Kennedy stood in Berlin and proclaimed to the besieged populace, "Ich bin ein Berliner!" This proclamation resounded around the world as the president responded to the Berlin Wall that East Germany had erected to divide East and West Berlin. As the Cold War continued, an ideological barrier between the East and West was extended across Europe, though the symbol of what became known as the "Iron Curtain" was always the Berlin Wall. Some 30 years later, President Ronald Reagan would respond to the Wall by encouraging his counterpart in the Soviet Union, "Mr. Gorbachev, tear down this wall!"[1] The Wall eventually came down in 1989, and in the party that ensued, U.S. celebrity David Hasselhoff performed his song "Freedom" atop the ruins to celebrate the barrier's destruction.[2]

The U.S. response to the Berlin Wall illustrates America's feelings about walls and barriers. As a country of immigrants, the United States was founded on an idea of openness and freedom. Few things undermine openness and freedom like a wall. In the 1880s, cattlemen and settlers fought "fence-cutter wars" over the fencing in of the plains and prairies.[3] This long history of consternation over fences and walls has led a majority of Americans to question the utility of constructing a wall on the southwest border of the United States. Some have gone so far as to label this the American Berlin Wall.[4] In March 2006, a U.S. representative from New York, Jose Serrano, spoke to a town hall meeting in his district about legislation authorizing the wall. He said, "The Sensenbrenner bill would build a wall along the 2,000-mile Mexican border after we told the Germans in 1980s to 'Tear down this wall.' We need more bridges, not walls."[5]

Yet sentimentality is not the only reason for so many Americans to believe this wall is a bad idea. Critics point out that the wall being built on the southwest border is ineffective, costs too much, causes environmental degradation, and is inherently racist.

## The border fence is an ineffective solution to illegal immigration.

"It's being built to appease middle America," Pat Ahumada, the mayor of Brownsville, Texas, suggested. Convinced that the border fence does not make sense, Ahumada said he believes the project has more to do with politics than real border security. In fact, he believes the fence will hurt his border town, making it more like a prison and scaring away tourists from Mexico and other U.S. towns.[6]

Ahumada is not alone. The mayors of several border towns oppose the border fence project. While they all have their own interests in stopping the fence, one thing unites them—their belief that the fence just won't work. Mayor Richard Cortez of McAllen, Texas, told CNN that the border fence is only a "speed bump" that may slow but will not stop illegal immigration.

Cortez said, "[i]t is a false sense of security. America will not be safe. America will continue to waste resources on something that is not going to work."[7]

One of the biggest problems with the border fence is that while it can limit immigration in specific areas, it just ends up shifting the flow to other points. While the United States has an almost 2,000-mile land border with Mexico, it has a 3,145-mile land border with Canada. This does not even take into account the 2,380-mile water boundary with Canada.[8] Coupled with the 12,479 miles of U.S. shoreline, 600 to 700 miles of fence do not seem as though it would be much of a deterrent to a dedicated foreigner trying to get into the United States.[9]

As with most bandage-style solutions to complex problems, a border fence does not address the underlying motivation for why people want to come to the United States in the first place. While some come for illegal reasons such as drug smuggling, most come to this country for the promise of a better life through economic advancement. Even in San Diego, where arguably the "most heavily fortified five miles of the border—all monitored from a command center" exists, illegal aliens still find a way over. San Diego sector chief Michael Fisher admits that when the fence goes up, "they can be up and over, in some cases in less than a minute." Ingenious methods of crossing have included everything from car carriers being used to drive over the fence to more than 20 tunnels that have been found going under the fence. Then there are the *coyotes*, immigrant smugglers who will get people into the United States—for a fee. In one CBS interview, a *coyote* in Tijuana, Mexico, boasted that he shuttled 40 people a week into the U.S. He explained, "You can build three or four fences along the border, but people will continue to cross because of the magnet of work."[10]

## Fencing the border will cost too much.

Being ineffective may not be the worst part of the border fence. The fence is also incredibly expensive. Based on the San Diego section of fence, projected costs for the border fence project are $1.2 billion. That is nearly $3 million for every mile of fence. This does not include the maintenance that will be required once the fence is up. Costs for lifetime maintenance are more than $50 billion![11] For $50 billion, initiatives could be set up that could solve the underlying economic motivations that underlie much of the illegal immigration from Mexico. In the case of Mexico, $50 billion would wipe out more than one-third of the country's debt, which ranks as one of the highest among industrialized nations.[12]

The really ridiculous part of this plan is that it does not even cover the entire southwestern border. At most it covers less than 700 miles out of the almost 2,000 miles of land border between the United States and Mexico. Such piecemeal fencing can hardly keep out those who are striving after a better life for themselves and their families. This does not take into account that professional people traffickers will quickly learn where the fence works and where the gaps are. This is not much protection for the $50 billion price tag.

The cost to some people is even greater. For those who own land on the border, the government is using its power of eminent domain to take the land so that the fence can be built. Even those who will not have their land taken from them may be separated from the richest area of irrigated land as the fence prevents them from using their property adjacent to the Rio Grande. For these farmers and ranchers, the cost of the fence is both emotionally wrenching and economically challenging.[13]

## A border fence will damage the environment.

For many, the cost of this fence is not merely a matter of dollar and cents but the damage done to the environment. Citizen groups, Indian tribes, and officials from adjacent towns are working together to highlight the environmental damage possible from this kind of massive obstruction, especially to delicate ecosystems. Two areas are of particular concern: endangered species and protected wildlife reserves.[14]

Of the many animals that roam across the southwestern deserts, some migratory animals need to be able to move from one locale to another for breeding and hunting reasons. Jaguars, pygmy owls, and pronghorns are no respecters of national boundaries, and all would be endangered if their migration routes were interfered with by installing large metal fencing for several miles at a stretch. These animals will also be stressed by the denuded "no-man's land" and Border Patrol roads that would occur between the two fences. When the wall gets to Texas, it is slated to cut through the Rio Grande Wildlife corridor. According to the environmental group No Border Wall:

> the border wall will slice through the heart of the Rio Grande wildlife corridor. US Fish & Wildlife has spent 30 years and $100 million to buy and revegetate lands to recreate habitat. Ocelots, numbering less than 100 and listed under the Endangered Species Act, live in the area's remaining habitat. Because so few are left in the U.S. they must have access to mates in Mexico to avoid inbreeding.[15]

Sensitive ecosystems along the border are also in danger. A 15-foot-high, solid-metal fence will affect wind patterns, animal trails, and other important aspects of a natural ecosystem. Coupled with the destruction of large swathes of vegetation to create the roads in between the fences, many of these unique and endangered environments are not likely to survive.[16]

The most troublesome aspect of this problem is that the federal government already had protections in place to make sure no one did exactly what Homeland Security is doing. Scores of environmental protection agencies and rules regulate how human presence can interact with the environment with the least amount of impact. Yet Secretary Michael Chertoff is determined to erect this wall and does not believe progress should be slowed. According to the activist group, he "bullied" Congress into passing the REAL ID Act of 2005:

which gave the Department of Homeland Security the power to waive all laws that might slow construction of a fence, and severely limited judicial review. Secretary of Homeland Security Michael Chertoff used his new power to "waive in their entirety" the Coastal Zone Management Act, the National Environmental Policy Act, the Endangered Species Act, the Migratory Bird Treaty Act, the Clean Water Act, the Clean Air Act, and the National Historic Preservation Act to extend triple fencing through the Tijuana River National Estuarine Research Reserve.[17]

Since gaining the power to nullify other federal regulations, Chertoff has used it three times to remove environmental protections that were slowing or might have slowed further construction of the fence.[18]

Concern over this situation is not limited to the U.S. side of the border. In November 2007, the Mexican government released a report intended to sway the U.S. government concerning the environmental impact of the border fence. The report charged that the border fence would harm the environment by threatening plant and animal life around the fence. The Mexican government encouraged the U.S. Congress to consider alternates methods of securing the border.[19]

## Building a wall on one border is inherently racist.

Not only is the border fence potentially damaging to the environment, it would damage the core values of the United States because it is inherently racist. The United States broke away from Great Britain by claiming such high ideals as recognizing "all men are created equal" and that they are endowed "with certain unalienable rights, that among these are Life, Liberty, and the Pursuit of Happiness." This same nation shames itself by trying to erect walls keeping out people who are striving after this very same American dream by pursuing their own life, liberty, and pursuit of happiness. Even more disturbing is the undercurrent of racism that seems to underlie much of the U.S. immigration policy. In February 2007, the New York University Republican club exemplified this kind of racism when it hosted a "find the immigrant" game at a city park. Boise State University College Republicans held "immigrant games" that included events involving climbing through a hole in a fence and showing illegal identification in order to win a free meal at a Mexican food restaurant.[20]

One of the claims behind why the United States needs a border fence is that it will help with national security. Since 9/11, it has become a common belief that the United States must secure its borders to avoid another terrorist attack. If that is the case, however, why are Congress and the Department of Homeland Security securing the *southern* border? All of the 9/11 hijackers entered the United States legally. The only terrorist who has been caught trying to cross the border into the United States was the so-called "millennium bomber," Ahmed Ressam. The interesting thing about his arrest was that he was caught crossing the *northern* U.S. border with Canada. In fact, there are no documented cases of any terrorist coming through the southern U.S. border. If national security were really the issue, the border fence should be constructed on the U.S.-Canada border, not the U.S.-Mexico border.[21]

Even if one were to ignore the ideological and moral problems with having a border policy that appears racist, there are practical implications as well. The United States needs good relations with our neighbors, especially if we are to get cooperation on finding some reasonable way of controlling the flow of people across the southern border. Former Mexico President Vicente Fox explained in an Associated Press interview, "To be so repressive isn't democratic or free. . . . To be putting up fences, chasing Mexicans, that isn't right . . . The U.S. needs better answers than repression, weapons and violence."[22]

## Summary

In a country that prides itself on promoting freedom and stopping repression around the world, the idea of putting up a wall to keep people out is antithetical to the core ideas of the U.S. With the same effort and energy we helped the Germans tear down their Berlin Wall, so we need to stop the wall being erected on the southern border of the United States.

The problems with the border wall are fourfold. First, it is ineffective. Erecting walls in certain locations will only funnel people into other areas, areas that could be more dangerous to both the illegal immigrants and to the environment. Second, the fence project is far too expensive. Billions of dollars are being spent on a fence that will not be effective when that money could go to economic relief that could help deal with the underlying economic motivations for illegal immigration. Third, the wall is damaging to the environment. Sensitive ecosystems are being permanently scarred with fencing that will lead to serious threats to species that are already in danger. Finally, the border fence is inherently racist. It targets only one nation while leaving the far larger northern and maritime borders unprotected. It also fails to protect the only border that has actually seen an apprehension of a terrorist suspect.

# Too Much Legal Immigration Is Damaging America's Economy and Society

W hen Gene Nelson, a fiber-optic engineer from Dallas, Texas, was dismissed from his Internet technology company in the summer of 2001 for cost-cutting reasons, the blow was hard enough. What made Nelson's blood boil was the revelation that his former employer was retaining a number of foreign "guest workers" on the payroll while laying off American citizens. These guest workers were nonimmigrants in the United States on temporary H-1B visas. "The H-1B program allows employers to cut Americans off the payroll who are making $90,000 or $100,000 a year and replace them with foreign workers making $30,000 to $40,000," Nelson told the *San Antonio Express-News*. "When you think about what happens when this is taken to their logical extreme, it's something that will destroy our economy."[1]

An H-1B visa does not allow its bearer to live and work permanently in the United States, but it does provide up to six years of residency for skilled foreign professionals—and it can provide a springboard for subsequent permanent residency. In theory, an employer is allowed to hire an H-1B worker only if it cannot find an American who is willing to take the job, and the company must advertise the position at the going market rate; in practice, critics allege, the system tilts in favor of cheap overseas labor. Corporations that are interested in keeping wage levels low and the workforce compliant have found plenty of ways to get around the law by advertising jobs in such a way that only H-1B holders will be willing or able to take them. Moreover, the younger and less financially and socially secure foreign workers who take these positions are less likely to rock the boat; employers can force them to work unpaid overtime or accept minimal benefits, knowing that there is little chance of an employee backlash. The guest workers are exploited by their bosses, but the biggest losers are the hardworking Americans who are suddenly told to vacate their desks while noncitizens working alongside them stay employed.

Some of the schemes concocted by corporations to abuse the H-1B system are breathtaking in their audacity. In one notorious case, a New Jersey–based insurance company asked 250 of its computer staff to train Indian contract workers who had obtained H-1Bs via a consultancy firm. Once the training was complete, the company promptly laid off all of its existing programmers and hired the Indians instead—at much lower salaries. The Department of Labor caught on to the scam and fined the consultancy firm more than $100,000 for its part, but the insurance company got away scot-free. [2] As Gene Nelson says, "Big business is what's driving all this, and I have zero faith any safeguards will stop it. Employers are addicted to the high profit margins they can get when they hire people on these visas."

Even if American companies stuck scrupulously to the law, would the situation be all that much better for American workers? The media focuses so much on the problem of illegal immigration that we can overlook how much damage *legal* immigration is causing to the country's economy and society. Of course, legal immigrants are by definition obeying U.S. laws and doing nothing wrong by coming to America, and we must resist any attempt to individually scapegoat them. Nonetheless, there is a good case to be made that too many legal immigrants are being permitted

## Immigration and the U.S. Computer Industry

Immigrant advocacy groups, as well as politicians who oppose immigration reform, frequently claim the nation's computer industry as one of large-scale immigration's success stories...yet these claims do not jibe with reality. Indeed, they are not even logical. To say that because a certain percentage of an industry has a certain ethnicity hardly justifies a claim that the industry "depends" on those particular ethnics. For instance, 40 percent of our nation's small motels happen to be run by immigrants from India; yet no one would leap to the conclusion that without Indians there would be no motels.

The true situation has very little to do with the industry's quest for "technical edge." During the 1980s, it became famous in Asia that the computer field was a route to emigration to the U.S., so many Asians flocked to the field. American employers were happy to hire them and sponsor them for green cards, because the foreigners represented cheap, compliant labor. Falcon International, a General Dynamics subcontractor, has even brazenly referred to the foreign nationals as having "indentured" status.

There is no question that some immigrant computer professionals have achieved prominence in their fields. For instance, An Wang, founder of Wang Laboratories, was a major contributor to early core memory technology. Our nation benefits greatly when employers bring truly exceptional foreign talents to the U.S., and this should be continued.

But at the same time, this view should not be extrapolated to foreign-born computer professionals in general. The vast majority are of ordinary abilities, hired into positions in which they perform ordinary work. In other words, it is incorrect to attribute the major technological advances of the industry to immigrants.

Source: Norman Matloff, "A Critical Analysis of the Economic Impacts of Immigration," July 1, 1995, updated March 20, 1999. http://www.cs.ucdavis.edu/~matloff/pub/Immigration/ImmigAndComputerIndustry/SVReport.html

to settle in the United States today. Immigration will always play a part in the American story, but it must not be allowed to increase to unprecedented levels; our standard of living, our safety, our environment, and our social fabric are at stake.

## Legal immigration is increasing at a rapid rate.

In 2007, more than 400,000 legal immigrants entered the United States and more than 600,000 aliens already in the country became legal permanent residents (LPR).[3] As the Federation for American Immigration Reform points out, that is enough people to found a city the size of Chicago.[4] This was not a one-time, unrepresentative figure. During the 2000s, the average annual intake figure was four times higher than the number of legal immigrants arriving in America in the 1960s (when the average was around 300,000 per year.) In fact, the period from 2000 to 2007 saw more than 10 million immigrants arrive in this country, the highest seven-year rate in U.S. history.[5] It is estimated that the foreign-born population of the United States, 37.9 million—or 11.5 percent of the total—will increase rapidly during the first half of the twenty-first century, assuming that today's liberal immigration rules remain unchange.[6]

Probably the most important reason for the increase in immigration numbers is so-called "chain migration." Under the regulations established in 1965, when the national quota system was abolished (see the Introduction for more details), a blood or marital tie to an American citizen became one of the key criteria for legal immigration. The principle behind this—that it is a good thing to reunite families—is an admirable one. What the reformers in the 1960s failed to take into account was the domino, or chain, effect that such a provision would create. Say a non–U.S. citizen marries a U.S. citizen. Under the law, the alien can legally settle in this country. So far, so good. Once the non–U.S. citizen has obtained permanent residency status, he or she can petition to have his or her parents allowed in. Then the parents can petition to have their other children enter the country, and then those children can petition to have *their* spouses and children enter . . . and so on. The effect is a never-ending series of immigrations, all perfectly legal but increasingly disconnected from the citizen who began the process. Chains such as these can become enormous. According to the Federation for American Immigration Reform's "Chain Migration" fact sheet, the number of successful applications for entry to the United States on family grounds has increased 13 times since the policy's introduction in 1965.[7]

# How Does Immigration Affect Black Americans?

The Cooke Elementary School in Washington, D.C.'s Adams-Morgan neighborhood—home to white yuppies, poor blacks and Central American immigrants—recently received a $1 million federal grant. The windfall has become a source not of celebration but of fierce dispute. The grant was awarded to make the school completely bilingual—and much of the outrage has come from black parents and teachers. (Latino parents are divided on the issue.) Black teachers fear they will be transferred because they don't speak Spanish. As for the parents, one mother told the *Washington Post*, "This is my neighborhood. My brothers and sisters and cousins went to Cooke, my kids go to Cooke, and I don't want to see the nature of the school changed."

The incident illustrates an important question about immigration that is being neglected in our emerging policy debate on the issue: How does immigration affect black Americans? Ask the man on the street this question, and he will tell you that immigrants are outcompeting blacks, and other Americans, on numerous fronts. Yet, in Washington policy circles, this common-sense view is far from self-evident. Even more to the point, the question itself seldom gets raised these days, even as immigration heats up as a public policy issue. The indifference of black leaders to this question is a separate issue unto itself—as is the obsessive tolerance of liberals who reject the question out of an abiding faith that because blacks and today's immigrants are all "people of color" their interests must be congruent. As for conservatives, whether pro- or anti-immigration, they remain oblivious to the possible negative consequences of having black Americans see

## U.S. workers suffer because of immigration.

Legal immigration affects the American economy in several complex ways. The defenders of high immigration quotas argue that the net effect is positive: Immigrants perform low-paying work that American citizens are unwilling to do, and they stimulate economic growth by grassroots entrepreneurship. There is definitely *some* truth to this. Because legal immigration has increased so quickly and indiscriminately in the past few

yet another group of newcomers move past them in the struggle for social and economic advancement.

When the impact of immigration on blacks has indeed been scrutinized, it has been through such a narrow lens that the resulting analyses miss the bigger picture. The terrain has been dominated by labor-market economists, who have found that, as a result of immigration, black wage rates and employment levels have either benefited or at least held steady. While such general findings may be technically valid, they often fail to capture the relatively localized impacts of immigrants on low-skilled urban labor markets.

Evidence from the 1990 Census shows significant migration from areas where new immigrants live. This migration, though often portrayed as occurring among affluent whites, has in fact been most pronounced among poverty-level whites, and significant among blacks. Research by William Frey at the University of Michigan reveals that between 1985 and 1990 almost 12 percent of poor whites and almost 5 percent of poor blacks left metropolitan Los Angeles. Such migrations have been even greater in other metropolitan areas, notably New York and Chicago. Frey observes that these migrations might explain the widespread findings that immigration hasn't hurt blacks economically. In any event, in L.A. and other cities, Latino immigrants now do dominate substantial segments of the service sector, such as janitorial jobs. While they may not have pushed blacks out of these positions, Latinos are sufficiently entrenched that blacks will probably have a hard time finding their way back in.

Source: Peter Skerry, "The Black Alienation," *New Republic*, January 30, 1995. http://heather. cs.ucdavis.edu/pub/Immigration/EffOnMinorities/Skerry.html

decades, however, the effect on ordinary Americans has become more and more negative. Immigrants are swelling welfare rolls and burdening the government budget; they are forcing down wages, putting otherwise employable U.S. citizens out of work; and they are displacing even highly skilled American workers from well-compensated positions in high-tech industries such as computer programming and information technology.

In theory, immigrants are not supposed to become a public responsibility: A condition of entry into the United States is that a citizen pledges to support an immigrant financially. The problem is that the minimum level of sponsorship only has to be 25 percent higher than the official poverty level—in other words, someone earning barely enough to keep himself or herself off welfare is allowed to sponsor an immigrant whom they cannot realistically hope to provide for.

In any case, the rules regarding sponsorship are rarely enforced. The result is that state governments spend an estimated $11 billion to $22 billion annually on welfare for immigrants. It is true that, in 1996, the welfare system was reformed to make it more difficult for immigrants to become a public burden immediately on arrival in the United States. Even with the tightening of the law, however, immigrants can claim food stamps, housing assistance, child-care services, Medicaid, and a host of other services from the moment of entry. After five years, they are eligible for federal means-tested public benefits ("means-tested" means that only people below a certain income are eligible). Because family-based chain migration takes almost no account of an immigrant's ability to fend for himself or herself, it is likely that the number of foreign-born residents permanently claiming welfare will increase.[8]

Norman Matloff noted in a 1995 paper that "Even many pro-immigration economists and immigrant advocates now concede that immigration does result in a significant degree of displacement of American workers, both U.S. natives and earlier-arriving immigrants. This displacement occurs both in low-skilled and high-skilled occupations. Minorities are particularly hard hit."[9] The last point is worth stressing. It is sometimes suggested that those who are against immigration are motivated by ethnic prejudice or outright racism; in fact, America's minority communities are often the most affected by legal immigration. By providing a surplus of low-wage competition, immigrants make it more difficult for, say, African Americans or American-born Latinos from poorer neighborhoods to seek out the jobs they need to improve their opportunities in life. Immigration hurts those who are most vulnerable to the fluctuations of the economy, the already disadvantaged and needy.

## Too many legal immigrants are a national security risk.

Most aliens who enter the United States do so for innocuous reasons—for short-term travel and tourism or for longer-term work or study. Whether their presence in such large numbers is a good thing for America as a whole is debatable, but at least their individual motives are innocent enough. A small number of aliens arrive here for far more sinister purposes, however. The two attacks on New York's World Trade Center—the first in 1993 and the second, far more devastating one in 2001—showed that a handful of aliens are willing to commit mass murder on U.S. soil in order to pursue their political goals. Their numbers might be tiny in comparison with the majority of peaceful foreign-born visitors and residents, but the damage they can do makes them a primary national security threat. We cannot ignore the relationship between immigration and terrorism any longer.

We also cannot ignore the reality that the greatest security threat comes from citizens of a relatively small number of countries. Prominent among these are high-risk nations such as Iran, Syria, North Korea, Pakistan, and Saudi Arabia. As a 2001 Center for Immigration Studies report says, "While it is absolutely essential that we not scapegoat immigrants, especially Muslim immigrants, we also must not overlook the most obvious fact:

the current terrorist threat to the United States comes almost exclusively from individuals who arrive from abroad."[10]

The problem of terrorism is an enormous one, but a start can be made by drastically reducing the loopholes open to aliens from high-risk areas who come to the United States temporarily. Student visas, for example, are a much-abused avenue of entry. Although foreign students are not supposed to remain in the United States longer than their term of study, it is relatively easy for them to overstay their legal residency and disappear into the community, sometimes with fake identification—which is just what several of the 9/11 hijackers did. If visas were awarded more scrupulously on the basis of risk, then opportunities to travel to America for malicious purposes would be limited. Congressman Ron Paul, who has campaigned to reduce the handout of visas to high-risk students, said in 2003 that our educational programs "should not serve as an easy revolving door that allows our worst enemies to live among us."[11]

## The environment suffers because of immigration.

Perhaps one of the most contentious immigration disputes of recent years has been its effect on the environment. The battle has split the venerable Sierra Club, the oldest and largest environmental protection society in the United States. Members are bitterly divided on the matter, and the debate within the club has become increasingly rancorous. "Many environmentalists are not willing to deal with this very important issue," says Ben Zuckerman, the founder of a group called Support U.S. Population Stabilization (SUSPS), which argues that immigration is exacerbating America's natural resource crisis.[12]

The United States consumes more resources than any other country in the world, and its population is increasing at a rate normally associated with developing countries such as India and China; this population bulge is largely caused by legal immigration. "Today's current world population harbors millions—if not billions—of people who are eager to enter the U.S.," SUSPS says on its Web site. "This degree of immigration would devastate our remaining open spaces and ecosystems and place an unacceptable burden on our infrastructure."[13] The environmental problems that are already facing North Americans—pollution of air and water supplies, deforestation, depletion of soil quality, and the destruction of rural land by urban and suburban development—are just going to get worse if the number of U.S. residents increases at the projected rate. The United States may be a large country, but there are limits on how many people it can absorb before resource management becomes impossible. We already know how unpredictable the nation's oil supply can be, given the political disturbances that have taken place in petroleum-exporting regions of the world such as the Middle East. What will happen in half a century, when another 100 million or more Americans—most of whom will be the product of immigration—drive their cars onto the country's interstates?

## Immigration is damaging to American—and world—society.

Immigration advocates frequently assert that "America is a land of immigration," implying that there is something un-American about reform of the current system. This is a flawed argument. Just because the United States has *historically* received a lot of immigrants does not mean that it must do so forever. This has been a land of many things, not all of them attractive: Slavery, racial discrimination, inequality, and injustice have marred the nation's history. We should not preserve habits or patterns of behavior simply because "that's the way we've always done it." The point of history is to learn and to move on. A century ago, the United States was an underpopulated country that could not provide its own labor needs. That is no longer the case. We should not be afraid to admit that the United States is a different place than it was at the time of Ellis Island and that immigration policies that might have made sense during the presidency of Theodore Roosevelt no longer apply.

It is true that American life has been enriched by immigration in the past, but it is not so clear that the largely unrestricted flow of legal aliens today will have the same positive result. As immigration has an increasingly damaging effect on the American economy, so tensions that will damage American *society* as well will emerge. The tolerance and pluralism of American democracy depends on a belief that we have common goals and aspirations, that whatever our differences on certain issues, all Americans are united in a fundamental way. An influx of foreign-born migrants who are visibly undermining wage levels and job opportunities for the rest will fracture this important social harmony. Economic competition among ethnic groups can only lead to mutual suspicion and anger, an outcome that is bad for everyone, native born and immigrant alike.

There is another factor in all this as well—the economic and social well-being of the countries that immigrants are leaving. Developing nations cannot afford the "brain drain" of talented, well-educated citizens who come to the United States in search of high-tech jobs. These countries need to expand their economic bases in order to provide for the welfare of their people, but the corporate and technological leaders that they need are being siphoned off by large U.S. companies, a situation that hurts American workers *and* the world's poor. This "lose-lose" result cannot be justified on any grounds. We should encourage gifted foreign students to come to American universities and gain knowledge to take home for the benefit of their own countries, but we do everyone a disservice by allowing them to stay in the United States, where their skills are lost to their own people.

## Summary

Immigration is going to play *some* kind of role in America's future; that seems certain. Whether for self-interested or compassionate reasons, there will always be a certain number of foreign-born residents settling permanently in the United States. In moderation, such a policy can only be beneficial. The problem with immigration today is that moderation has been abandoned; rather than enforcing sensible, manageable quotas, the United States has opened the floodgates to a more or less unrestricted surge of aliens who are placing an impossible burden on the nation's economic, cultural, and political framework. It is not "immigrant bashing" to point out the failures of current policy. On the contrary, those people who sincerely want the American immigration system to thrive and for new citizens to be absorbed successfully into U.S. society should realize how much damage we are doing by our thoughtless abandonment of visa and naturalization restrictions.

# Immigrants Are a Vital Economic and Social Asset to the United States

Dominic Gambino always wanted to come to America. While growing up on a small farm in Sicily in the 1950s, he dreamed of the United States as the fabled land of opportunity. In 1968, he got his chance to come here when he took a job at a Chicago tool and dye factory where his brother worked. Gambino's initial prospects were not good. He spoke no English and had little money and few connections. He worked two jobs and went to night school to learn English. "It was really rough," he remembers, "but I was glad to have the work and my wife. In my mind it was always 'I've got to make my own business.'"

Initially, Gambino thought he would save some money and then return to Sicily. As he and his wife, Marion, settled down and had children, however, their attachment to the Chicago area deepened. Then he and his nephew borrowed enough money to open a grocery. Gambino continued to work at the factory during the day to pay the bills, and, within four years, he had paid off his loans and was making a small profit. A second location was opened, and then a third. Now the Gambinos own five groceries, employ many fellow Chicagoans, and have helped revitalize some long-abandoned retail sites in the city. Gambino is thankful for his success, which he owes to commitment and honest labor: "We work hard, a lot of hours, a lot of honesty. My girls love to work in the business. We help the employees; we help the community, the church and the schools." As far as Sicily is concerned, he continues to visit his family there on occasion, but his home now is the United States: "My heart is here. My family is here."[1]

Dominic Gambino's story is typical of the American immigrant experience. People from around the world have been coming to the United States for centuries in search of basic ideals: religious and political liberty, economic fortune, and the chance to remake their lives in a land that offers unparalleled opportunities. These immigrants have not just gained from the encounter, they have also enriched America as a whole, both materially and culturally. It is the sheer effort and willingness of people such as the Gambinos to undergo short-term hardships in the interests of their long-term welfare that have, literally, made the United States.

Why, then, do some Americans see immigration as a threat rather than a blessing? Part of the answer may be racial or ethnic hostility, but on the whole it probably has more to do with basic misunderstandings about the impact immigrants have on American life. If people are constantly told that immigrants are arriving in unprecedented numbers, stealing their jobs, overpopulating their country, and damaging their security and their way of life, then it is only natural that they will reject the immigrant presence.

In fact, none of these claims are true. The hordes of foreign interlopers that are conjured up by critics of immigration have more to do with hype than reality. The immigrant contribution to economic growth is consistently positive, and the national-security implications of immigration are vastly overblown. There is little evidence that the United States is facing an imminent environmental disaster caused by immigrant numbers. Nor is American society teetering on the brink of anarchy because of immigrants. To get away from the shock headlines and gain a more sophisticated understanding of immigration, we need to look at each one of these issues separately.

## The increase in legal immigration is exaggerated.

"For nearly two generations, great numbers of persons utterly unable to earn their living . . . and others who were, from widely different causes, unfit to be members of any decent community, were admitted to our ports without challenge or question. . . . The question to-day is . . . of protecting the American rate of wages, the American standard of living, and the quality of American citizenship from degradation through the tumultuous access of vast throngs of [the] ignorant and brutalized."[2] This quote could come from the pen of a present-day critic of immigration. In fact, it was written more than 100 years ago, and the author was criticizing the arrival of immigrants from Italy, Russia, and other parts of Eastern and Southern Europe—people whose grandchildren and great-grandchildren are now as thoroughly American as anyone else. For generations, anti-immigration activists have been warning about the "avalanche" of foreigners who are going to destroy the United States as we know it. Strangely, this imminent disaster never seems to arrive. The current rash of scare stories about immigration is just one more example of this.

The present-day rate of immigration to the United States is not unprecedented at all. It is true that the number of foreign-born residents of the United States is a little higher than it was 40 years ago—it stands at about 11 percent—but this is still lower than the 14.7 percent of Americans who were naturalized in 1910. The only reason that today's numbers look so much higher than those of a century ago is that the total population is much larger than it was then, and so, naturally, the total number of immigrants is larger, even if it represents a smaller percentage of the whole. If anything, the immigration "problem" today is smaller than it was before World War I.[3]

## American workers benefit from immigration.

One of the most mischievous claims about immigrants is that they are a drain on the American economy, stealing jobs and burdening the public welfare system. Actually, the United States gains enormously from the industriousness and hard work of its immigrant population: As the free-market research center the Cato Institute put it in its 2003 recommendations to Congress, "Immigration gives America an economic edge in the global economy. Immigrants bring innovative ideas and entrepreneurial spirit to the United States, most notably in Silicon Valley and other high-technology centers. They provide business contacts with other markets, enhancing America's ability to trade and invest profitably abroad."[4] The figures are clear. In 2000, immigrants established 18 percent of all small businesses in the United States—the type of businesses that create most jobs overall—and they are more likely than native-born residents to be self-employed or to start their own companies. In total, immigrants today pay between $90 billion and $140 billion in taxes annually (while receiving only a fraction of this in return as welfare) and earn $240 billion toward the national economy.[5]

Business entrepreneurs such as Jenny Ming, the CEO of clothing retailer Old Navy, and Intel Corporation founder Andrew Grove are particularly impressive immigrant role models, but they are just spectacular examples of the humbler success stories that take place in America's downtowns, commercial parks, and malls all the time. Dominic Gambino's Chicago groceries are replicated in spirit across the United States, from the restaurants of San Francisco's Chinatown to the Indian hoteliers who run motor lodges along the Northeast's busy Interstate 95 corridor. Instead of complaining about the supposed damage that immigrants are doing to the economy, Americans should be thankful for the injection of talent and industry that resident aliens bring with them. It is their can-do attitude and their willingness to forgo temporary luxuries for long-term gain that create jobs for everyone.

# Leading Immigrant-Founded Venture-Backed Public Companies Ranked By Employment

| Company | Immigrant-Born Founder Or Cofounder | Country of Birth | Employees (FY 2005) | Industry |
|---|---|---|---|---|
| Intel Corporation | Andy Grove | Hungary | 99,900 | Semiconductor and Related Device Manufacturing |
| Solectron Corporation | Winston Chen | Taiwan | 53,000 | Bare Printed Circuit Board Manufacturing |
| Sanmina-SCI Corporation | Jure Sola<br>Milan Mandaric | Bosnia<br>Croatia | 48,621 | Bare Printed Circuit Board Manufacturing |
| Sun Micro-systems, Inc. | Andreas Bechtolsheim<br>Vinod Khosla | Germany<br><br>India | 31,000 | Electronic Computer Manufacturing |
| eBay, Inc. | Pierre Omidyar | France | 12,600 | Electronic Auctions |
| Yahoo! Inc. | Jerry Yang | Taiwan | 9,800 | Web Search Portals |
| Life Time Fitness, Inc. | Bahram Akradi | Iran | 9,500 | Fitness and Rec-reational Sports Centers |
| Tatra Tech, Inc. | Henri Hodara | France | 7,200 | Engineering Services |
| UTStarcom, Inc. | Ying Wu | China | 6,300 | Telephone Apparatus Manufacturing |
| Google, Inc. | Sergey Brin | Russia | 5,680 | Web Search Portals |
| Kanbay International, Inc. | Raymond J. Spencer<br>Dileep Nath<br>John Patterson | Australia<br><br>India<br>Canada | 5,242 | Computer Systems Design Services |
| Cadence Design Systems, Inc. | Alberto Sangiovanni-Vincentelli | Italy | 5,000 | Software Publishers |

| Company | Immigrant-Born Founder Or Cofounder | Country of Birth | Employees (FY 2005) | Industry |
|---|---|---|---|---|
| Juniper Networks, Inc. | Pradeep Sindhu | India | 4,415 | Telephone Apparatus Manufacturing |
| Watson Pharmaceuticals, Inc. | Allen Chao | Taiwan | 3,844 | Pharmaceutical |
| Parametric Technology Corporation | Samuel Geisberg | Russia | 3,751 | Software Publishers |
| Pediatrix Medical Group, Inc. | Roger Medel | Cuba | 3,013 | Offices of Physicians (except Mental Health Specialists) |
| NVIDIA Corporation | Jen-Hsun Huang | Taiwan | 2,737 | Semiconductor and Related Device Manufacturing |
| Salton, Inc. | Lewis Salton | Poland | 2,466 | Electric Housewares and Household Fan Manufacturing |
| Lam Research Corporation | David Lam | China | 2,200 | Semiconductor Machinery Manufacturing |
| WebEx Communications, Inc. | Subrah S. Iyar | India | 2,091 | Software Publishers |

Employment reflects 2005 worldwide total

Sources: Company 10-K filings and Hoover's

Stuart Anderson and Michaela Platzer, *American Made: The Impact of Immigrant Entrepreneurs and Professionals on U.S. Competitiveness*, National Venture Capital Association, Accessed June 2, 2008. http://www.nvca.org/pdf/AmericanMadde_study.pdf

## Stigmatizing immigrants as a national security risk is discrimination.

The economic complaints about legal immigrants go back many years, and the security complaints—the accusations that foreign-born residents are conspiring to injure the United States—are old too, much older than recent terrorist alarms might suggest. Shortly after the 1917 Russian Revolution, there was a prolonged "Red Scare" throughout the United States. Excited journalists and politicians claimed that tens of thousands of "dangerous, destructive, and anarchistic" Russian-born residents were planning to overthrow America's democratic system in the same way that the czarist government had been toppled in Russia. The charges were ridiculous, but that did not stop the persecution of many legal immigrants and the abuse of their civil rights. The campaign was fueled by ignorance, panic, and prejudice, in particular the irrational fear of strangers from a certain scapegoat country that was very much in the news. Today the target of anti-immigrant rhetoric has changed from Russia to the Middle East, but the emotions that fueled the Red Scare are as much in evidence now as then.[6]

Terrorism is a real problem, but it is one that transcends lazy stereotypes about nationality. It is easily forgotten that, when the first reports about the 1995 Oklahoma City bombing began circulating in the media, it was taken for granted that the perpetrators must have been Arab or other Islamic terrorists. Only when the truth emerged that two white, Christian, U.S.-born extremists were the real criminals did the wave of finger-pointing subside. It is true that many terrorists do hail from high-risk countries such as Pakistan and Saudi Arabia, but others are not so easy to identify. Richard Reid, the so-called "Shoe Bomber" who attempted to blow up a transatlantic air flight in 2001, was every bit as dangerous as the 9/11 attackers, but he was a natural-born citizen of Great Britain, America's closest ally in the War on Terror. How would selective restrictions on high-risk nations have prevented Reid from attempting to carry out his plans? The key to tackling terrorism is the precise targeting of specific criminals, not the arbitrary harassment of people whose only crime is to have the wrong passport or the wrong skin color.

## The natural environment does not suffer because of immigration.

Among the more provocative claims of anti-immigration campaigners is that America's natural environment is suffering because of incoming foreign residents. This is a controversial issue partly because the facts are so unclear and disputed and also because environmentalists tend to come from the left end of the political spectrum, which has traditionally been more tolerant of high immigration levels than the right end is. The environmental impact of immigration has become an issue that transcends standard political divisions in the United States, and some on the left believe that it has been deliberately pushed by conservatives in order to split the liberal camp. Regardless of their motives, "green" activists are missing the point by attacking immigrants for environmental damage. There *are* real and urgent risks to America's natural resources, but these cannot be blamed on immigration.

It is sometimes argued that the United States is too overpopulated to allow further immigration: there is no room at the inn, so to speak. The problem is that any definition of "overpopulation" is inherently subjective; in principle, an enormous amount of people can live in a very small area as long as basic food and living needs are met. As one environmentalist pointed out in 1990, "The world's 5.3 billion inhabitants could fit on the island of Tasmania [off southern Australia] if they were prepared to have a density equivalent to that of downtown Manhattan and the technology to service such a residential mega-metropolis."[7] The global population has increased somewhat since then, but the point remains the same: There is no absolute measure of overpopulation; we have to decide for ourselves how many people we regard as acceptable within a given space. When you consider that the number of U.S. citizens per square kilometer is about one-quarter that of the

## "The Global Battle for Talent and People"

America's strength lies in its openness and dynamic character. Current concerns about the U.S. economy should not distract from an understanding that in the long term America's economic success requires the nation to attract 1) skilled professionals from across the globe to increase the competitiveness of American companies and 2) workers at the lower end of the skill spectrum to fuel the growth of the U.S. labor force, filling jobs created by the aging of the population.

An extensive review of government, academic and private-sector materials and research reveals the following findings in this report:

- With current levels of immigration, the U.S. labor force will grow 18.9 percent by 2030, while countries with more restrictive immigration policies such as Japan, Germany and Italy will see their adult working populations decline by 15 percent or more. Immigration is the crucial factor in determining whether the United States labor force will experience growth or become stagnant. This U.S. labor growth, led by immigration, will be a key to economic growth and the funding of health and retirement benefits for baby boomers....

- A large drop in spending on computers and related hardware and slower growth in spending on software would appear to be the primary reasons for job difficulties in certain high technology sectors, not the entry of foreign-born professionals.

- Immigrant professionals contribute significantly to job creation in the United States, with Indian and Chinese entrepreneurs alone heading 29 percent of Silicon Valley's technology businesses. Collectively these companies accounted for $19.5 billion in sales and 72,839 jobs in 2000, according to the University of California at Berkeley.

- Foreign-born individuals are key contributors to innovation, making up 28 percent of all individuals with Ph.D.s in the United States who are engaged in research and development in science and engineering.

- Contrary to concerns that foreign-born professionals in the United States are "cheap labor" and undercut the wages of U.S. professionals, data indicate that foreign-born professionals working in the United States actually earn more than their native counterparts when controlled for age and the year in which a science or engineering degree is earned, according to the National Science Foundation....

- An examination of the data reveals that H-1B totals do not show rampant hiring by U.S. employers without regard to market conditions. In fact, H-1B hiring appears to rise and fall with economic conditions, as one would expect. In 2001, the number rose to 164,000. However, in FY [fiscal year] 2002, the number dropped by half—to 79,100, well below the 195,000 ceiling and equaling approximately 0.058 percent of the total U.S. labor force.

- Armed with new powers, as well as additional funding derived from employers' H-1B fees, the Department of Labor has increased enforcement of H-1B rules. Despite this increased enforcement, the number of serious violations remains low both in total and as a percentage of H-1B petitions approved, indicating that abuse is not widespread. In 2001, only 9 violations were deemed willful or requiring debarment, while there were 7 such violations in 2002.

- In addition to billions of dollars paid by U.S. employers in training their own employees and taxes for education, fees paid by U.S. employers to hire foreign-born professionals on H-1B visas have totaled more than $692 million over the past 5 years and will exceed $1 billion if the current fee continues for at least two more years. These fees have helped provide training to more than 55,600 U.S. workers and have funded scholarships for more than 12,500 U.S. students in science and engineering.

Curtailing legal immigration to the United States or further impeding the flow of skilled foreign professionals to America will hurt the nation's competitiveness and its leadership in the world. Such actions would slow U.S. labor-force growth, inhibit innovation inside the United States, reduce job growth, and encourage increased efforts to outsource and place overseas high technology jobs and centers for research and development. In addition, other nations appear poised to accept skilled foreign professionals in greater numbers to enhance the competitiveness of their industries. While we must take appropriate measures to protect U.S. security, an approach that facilitates the lawful entry of workers at the lower end of the skills spectrum and openness to skilled professionals at the high end will help America prosper in the global battle for talent and people.

Source: Stuart Anderson, "The Global Battle for Talent and People," *Immigration Policy Focus*, September 2003. http://www.ailf.org/ipc/ipf0903.asp

population density of Indonesia, one-ninth that of Great Britain, and one-eighteenth that of South Korea, the United States doesn't look nearly so crowded. In fact, many of our states are remarkably empty. According to the 1990 U.S. Census, New Mexico has 4.8 residents per square kilometer of territory, North Dakota 3.6, and Montana a mere 2.1 (compared with more than 20,000 in New York City).[8] With low densities such as these, some regions of the United States have major infrastructural dilemmas: Their tiny populations are not able to support adequate health and emergency services, for example. Some of America's problems are caused by too *few* people, not too many.

This is not to deny that the fate of the environment is a genuine and increasingly pressing issue. The problems of resource depletion, deforestation, and so on are above all *global* problems, though; they cannot simply be deferred by closing the gates to immigrants and pretending that the rest of the world does not exist. Rather than rejecting people from abroad, we should absorb their brainpower and imagination to help solve the environmental dilemmas that ultimately threaten us all, regardless of place of origin.

## Immigration enriches American—and world—society.

It seems a little strange to argue that American culture and society, which have been built up over centuries by the overlapping contributions of waves of foreign immigrants, is now under threat precisely *because* of immigration. The argument is made nonetheless, and it needs to be answered. Some critics allege that the problem today is distinct because the old "melting pot" has been abandoned: Immigrants no longer successfully assimilate into mainstream American life as they used to and are balkanizing our society into separate enclaves that cause disunity and intolerance. This view probably owes more to misplaced nostalgia than to hard reality. As discussed in the following chapters on English language policy, the United States was probably *more* ethnically chaotic a century ago than it is now. The influence of modern American pop culture is so vast that people are inevitably drawn into it, whether they realize it or not. Is there any teenager in America, regardless of where he or she was born or what language he or she originally spoke, who doesn't know who Britney Spears or Hannah Montana is? Worrying about a breakdown in social communication when our lives are increasingly dominated by an all-consuming mass media seems beside the point.

On a more down-to-earth level, immigrants have had an enormously welcome impact on the American landscape. The influx of new residents keeps important downtown areas of cities such as New York's Manhattan alive and energetic; immigrants revitalize dying neighborhoods and provide the crucial tax base for the aging native-born populations of large urban areas. The effect of immigration on the nations that they have left behind is positive. Although "new Americans" overwhelmingly show strong allegiance to their adopted country—a large number of immigrants join the American military forces—they maintain material and sentimental links to their original homelands. They supply financial support to relatives abroad, which, in the case of developing countries, can be an important source of national income. Immigration is not always one-way either: Sometimes second-generation children who have grown up in the United States but who are curious about their ethnic origins return to study or work in their parents' native land, providing valuable educational or technical assistance to those places and encouraging cooperation across frontiers.

## Summary

"The truth," said former New York Governor Mario Cuomo in 1993, "is that the challenges we face as a nation have not been imported by our immigrants, nor would they disappear if we could only succeed in sealing our borders for good—even if that were possible. In fact, there is good reason to believe that some of the problems we should take most seriously as a people—from the decline in our economic competitiveness to the decay of our community values—are problems that the new immigrants can help us solve."[9] As the descendant of Italian immigrants himself, Cuomo's successful political career is testament to the promise of the immigrant experience and the benefits it can bring all Americans. Rather than use immigration as a cheap and easy way to transfer the blame for our social and economic ills, which have far more complex origins, U.S. citizens should embrace the possibilities of our multiethnic tradition and recognize the many advantages that immigration brings us, in practical as well as culturally enriching ways.

# English Should Be the Official Language of the United States

I f a Klingon ever happens to make his way to the United States, he doesn't have to worry about brushing up on his English first. At least, that appears to be one of the results of Executive Order (EO) 13166, a decree that President Bill Clinton signed in 2000 requiring all federally funded institutions to provide services in *any* language requested, no matter how obscure. When local government officers in the mental health department of Multnomah County, Oregon, drew up a plan for accommodating this new policy, they calculated that they would need the ability to translate in more than 50 languages—including Klingon, a fictitious alien dialect invented by the writers of the *Star Trek* sci-fi series. "We have to provide information in all the languages our clients speak," said Jerry Jelusich, a spokesman for the county Department of Human Services; the fact that Klingons do not exist was beside the point as far as EO 13166 was concerned.[1]

After a couple of days of this story circulating in the media, embarrassed Multnomah County officials announced that the need for a Klingon translator had been dropped. They blamed a well-meaning but "overzealous" attempt to interpret the requirements of the executive order. Some legal observers have argued that EO 13166 *does* in fact require government-assisted bodies to provide Klingon translation—and the person making the request does not even have to be able to speak Klingon! According to attorney Barnaby Zall, "The Oregon hospital is required to hold up 'I speak' cards to enable clients to indicate their language preference. The person points to 'Klingon.' Do you have to investigate further or just accept it?"[2] Because any delay in providing services to such a client could jeopardize the institution's federal funding, its staff would probably just have to take the person's claim on trust, even if that person couldn't really speak a word of Klingon. The potential for absurd, expensive, and time-wasting abuse of such a policy is vast.

The reason bad ideas such as EO 13166 exist is because the United States never formally made English its official language of government. English is the language most commonly used in day-to-day conversation and business throughout America, and, at the local level, it has been given some kind of official ranking in 23 states, but it has never been recognized by the federal government with the special status it so clearly deserves. Does this really matter? Yes, for both practical and symbolic reasons, it matters a lot. The provision of non-English documentation and translation is costly and squanders public resources that could be better used elsewhere. More important, the English language is one of the cultural keystones of American society: It gives U.S. citizens a common frame of reference and understanding and provides way of uniting peoples who come from different ethnic backgrounds. The United States is already fractured enough economically, geographically, and racially. If we do not learn to value our common language, we will become a people who literally cannot comprehend one another.

## We need an official English policy today as never before.

Many Americans might be surprised to discover that English is not, and has never been, the official language of the United States. Why, they might ask, didn't the Founding Fathers introduce such a clause in the Constitution? The answer is that multilingualism didn't seem to be a big problem in the age of Washington, Jefferson, and Franklin. In the early years of the republic, the majority of free American citizens hailed from the British Isles and so spoke English as their native tongue. It was taken for granted that government business in the United States would be conducted in that language. Even eighteenth-century African Americans, most of whom were slaves, learned and spoke English despite their different ethnic origins.

Fair enough, a critic might answer, but what about the nineteenth and early twentieth centuries, when large numbers of immigrants from non-English-speaking parts of the world arrived on American shores? If an "Official English" policy is so important for national unity, why wasn't it introduced then? It is true that the United States didn't *officially* recognize English as its language of government during the 1800s and early 1900s, but in *practice* it did. Immigrants arriving at Ellis Island or one of the country's other ports or border stations knew that they would have to learn English in order to make a successful life in America; refusing to do so wasn't a realistic option. That may have caused some temporary hardship for first-generation immigrants, but in the long run it was in everyone's best interests. The "melting pot" theory worked: Through the acquisition of English skills, new U.S. citizens became part of a single culture in which they could make their ideas and opinions known to everyone. This did not mean abandoning all traces of native customs and traditions. Far from it. We can see how vibrant and multitextured American society has become by the introduction of Spanish architecture, Chinese and Italian cooking, and Brazilian music, for example. There is no contradiction between

As large numbers of immigrants from non-English-speaking parts of the world continue to arrive in the United States, the government has made efforts to accommodate them by providing services in multiple languages. Public schools face a particular challenge in educating students who do not speak English. Above, a teacher instructs students in her English as a second language (ESL) class.

preserving cultural roots and embracing a *lingua franca*—a common tongue—such as English.

The problem in recent years is that the U.S. government (at all levels) has been making it easier for immigrants to avoid learning English by providing translation services and documentation in many other languages. Instructions for the 2000 U.S. census were available in 50 different vernaculars, from Albanian to Yiddish. This might *seem* like a generous or enlightened policy, but the result is not harmony; rather it is the opposite—increasing linguistic isolation across the country, with all the unfortunate consequences that entails. In Ohio in the past decade, the number of Spanish speakers has jumped by half, to more than 200,000, and more than one-third of them admit that they cannot speak English well.[3] As of 2003, a quarter of the Hispanic population of Hartford, Connecticut, could speak little or no English at all; the city has made so many concessions to these Spanish-only speakers that there is little incentive for them to ever acquire English. "We've become a Latin city, so to speak," says the mayor. "It's a sign of things to come."[4] English is under serious threat in communities such as these.

## Not having an official English policy is needlessly expensive.

A multilinguistic policy is indefensible on grounds of cost alone. Accommodating all the languages spoken in the United States today, as measures such as EO 13116 require, would be enormously expensive. It is estimated that there are between 330 and 430 foreign dialects—everything from Abkhaz (originating in the Caucasus mountains of southern Russia) to Zapoteco (a native language of Mexico), and not forgetting Klingon, of course—used in America. Imagine the duplication involved in converting all government materials into this vast array of languages and the resulting price tag. The experience of Canada, which has an official English-French bilingual policy, provides some sobering calculations. From 1980 to 1990, it cost the Canadian government $6.7 billion to translate its English documentation into French and vice-versa. The U.S. has a population 10 times that of Canada and a corresponding paperwork problem 10 times as large. Based on that figure, if the United States were to take the multilingual mandate of EO 13166 seriously, it would have to spend $10 billion a year—a sum equal to the 2004 budget of the Treasury Department—doing nothing more than translating documents![5]

Critics might respond that only a few key languages, such as Spanish and Chinese, have to be given special treatment. Even leaving aside the philosophical injustice of this—why should an immigrant from the Dominican Republic or Hong Kong be given arbitrary advantages over someone from, say, Nigeria or

Finland?—there is the issue of cost. Bilingual education, in which immigrant students are taught in their native language rather than in English, is an important example. California has more than 1.3 million students enrolled in bilingual programs, mostly involving Spanish. This costs the state $5 billion a year, money it could spend on other important projects.[6] This is aside from the

## "Treat Hispanics Like Americans"

Bush Administration officials interested in immigration and language policy would do well to ponder [political prisoner] Li Shaomin, whose Communist Chinese captors seized his passport and told him: "This will do you no good. You may have an American passport, but you're not a real American, and never will be."

This is the same message—"you're not a real American and never will be"—that the professional ethnic activists have persuaded the American government to send to all of our Hispanic citizens.

Thanks to federal and state language policies, families with Spanish names are treated as though they were illiterate in the English language. They receive letters from schools and government agencies in their "native" Spanish—even if their family has been in America for generations.

Bilingual-education programs say to Hispanic parents: "your children aren't real Americans and never will be." Bilingual education ensures Hispanic children will grow up to be second-class citizens because such programs keep Hispanic children from learning English when they are young and can do so most easily.

Even the *Washington Post* editorial page confessed: "the bilingual education offered in most parts of the country does not promote English fluency.... [I]t seems likely that students would learn more English if they were immersed in it."

...Hispanics are not an undifferentiated mass awaiting instructions from their self-appointed leaders in Washington. There are a good many Hispanics who proudly salute the Stars and Stripes rather than the flag of Mexico.... While the continued existence of "Hispanic rights" groups like La Raza and LULAC depends on convincing Hispanics that they will never be real Americans, [the U.S. government] should not follow their lead.

Source: Jim Boulet Jr., "Assimilation, Not Amnesty," *National Review Online*, August 21, 2001. http:// www.nationalreview.com/comment/comment-boulet082101.shtml

fact that the effectiveness of this expensive educational system is highly suspect.

## An official English policy would help immigrants.

Advocates of Official English are sometimes accused of being "bigots seeking to roll back civil rights advances" or "nativists trying to fan animosity toward immigrants."[7] This is nonsense. The chief beneficiaries of English as an official language would be immigrants themselves.

For some time, it has been clear that immigrants to the United States who do not rapidly acquire English language skills are at a grave disadvantage economically and socially. A 1992 study found that non-English-speaking immigrants earn, on average, 17 percent less than English-speaking immigrants of similar education and experience.[8] The inability to speak English can be dangerous, too: Hispanic workers have a 23 percent higher fatality rate from work-related injuries than other ethnic groups, largely because of misunderstood safety instructions and warnings.[9] Tragic medical mistakes have also resulted from language barriers between doctors and patients. In one analysis of translation errors at a pediatrics clinic, researchers found that the official interpreters made 231 errors, more than half of which could have resulted in serious diagnostic or treatment mistakes. These included telling a patient to take her antibiotic prescription for 2 days rather than 10, omitting important information about drug allergies, and giving faulty advice to mothers about their children's illnesses, which could have proven fatal.[10]

By not encouraging immigrants to learn English, the government is doing nothing to prevent these dangerous problems. The bilingual education of immigrant children only perpetuates their difficulties and inequalities. Hoover Institution Fellow Peter Duignan's survey of Hispanic students concluded that "[Bilingualism] is ineffective, keeps students too long in Spanish-only classes, and slows the learning of English and assimilation into American society. High dropout rates for Latino students, low graduation rates from high schools and colleges have imprisoned

## THE LETTER OF THE LAW

# Extracts from the English Language Unity Act of 2007 (Proposed)

### A BILL

To declare English as the official language of the United States, to establish a uniform English language rule for naturalization, and to avoid misconstructions of the English language texts of the laws of the United States, pursuant to Congress' powers to provide for the general welfare of the United States and to establish a uniform rule of naturalization under article I, section 8, of the Constitution.

*Be it enacted by the Senate and House of Representatives of the United States of America in Congress assembled,*

### SECTION 1. SHORT TITLE.

This Act may be cited as the 'English Language Unity Act of 2007'.

### SEC. 2. FINDINGS.

The Congress finds and declares the following:

(1) The United States is comprised of individuals from diverse ethnic, cultural, and linguistic backgrounds, and continues to benefit from this rich diversity.

(2) Throughout the history of the United States, the common thread binding individuals of differing backgrounds has been the English language.

(3) Among the powers reserved to the States respectively is the power to establish the English language as the official language of the respective States, and otherwise to promote the English language within the respective States, subject to the prohibitions enumerated in the Constitution of the United States and in laws of the respective States.

### CHAPTER 6—OFFICIAL LANGUAGE

*Sec. 161. Official language of the United States*

The official language of the United States is English.

*Sec. 162. Preserving and enhancing the role of the official language*

Representatives of the Federal Government shall have an affirmative obligation to preserve and enhance the role of English as the official language of the Federal Government. Such obligation shall include encouraging greater opportunities for individuals to learn the English language.

*Sec. 163. Official functions of Government to be conducted in English*

(a) Official Functions—The official functions of the Government of the United States shall be conducted in English.

(b) Scope—For the purposes of this section, the term 'United States' means the several States and the District of Columbia, and the term 'official' refers to any function that (i) binds the Government, (ii) is required by law, or (iii) is otherwise subject to scrutiny by either the press or the public.

(c) Practical Effect—This section shall apply to all laws, public proceedings, regulations, publications, orders, actions, programs, and policies, but does not apply to—

(1) teaching of languages;

(2) requirements under the Individuals with Disabilities Education Act;

(3) actions, documents, or policies necessary for national security, international relations, trade, tourism, or commerce;

(4) actions or documents that protect the public health and safety;

(5) actions or documents that facilitate the activities of the Bureau of the Census in compiling any census of population;

(6) actions that protect the rights of victims of crimes or criminal defendants; or

(7) using terms of art or phrases from languages other than English.

*Sec. 164. Uniform English language rule for naturalization*

(a) Uniform Language Testing Standard- All citizens should be able to read and understand generally the English language text of the Declaration of Independence, the Constitution, and the laws of the United States made in pursuance of the Constitution.

(b) Ceremonies- All naturalization ceremonies shall be conducted in English.

*(continues)*

*(continued)*

*Sec. 165. Rules of construction*

Nothing in this chapter shall be construed—

(1) to prohibit a Member of Congress or any officer or agent of the Federal Government, while performing official functions, from communicating unofficially through any medium with another person in a language other than English (as long as official functions are performed in English);

(2) to limit the preservation or use of Native Alaskan or Native American languages (as defined in the Native American Languages Act);

(3) to disparage any language or to discourage any person from learning or using a language; or

(4) to be inconsistent with the Constitution of the United States.

## SEC. 5. IMPLEMENTING REGULATIONS.

The Secretary of Homeland Security shall, within 180 days after the date of enactment of this Act, issue for public notice and comment a proposed rule for uniform testing English language ability of candidates for naturalization, based upon the principles that—

(1) all citizens should be able to read and understand generally the English language text of the Declaration of Independence, the Constitution, and the laws of the United States which are made in pursuance thereof; and

(2) any exceptions to this standard should be limited to extraordinary circumstances, such as asylum.

Source: http://www.govtrack.us/congress/billtext.xpd?bill=h110-997

Spanish speakers at the bottom of the economic and educational ladder in the United States."[11] A policy that is ostensibly designed to help non-English-speaking immigrants in fact keeps them trapped in a linguistic ghetto.

Of course, Official English advocates recognize that a few concessions to multilingualism will always have to be made for reasons of public safety or criminal justice. Emergency assistance should be available to non-English speakers, for example, and translators should be available to allow immigrants to testify in court and understand the proceedings. The use of foreign languages in *private* life would be unaffected by an Official English law; no one is suggesting that the personal lives of citizens would be investigated by some kind of language police. The point behind an English-only law for government would be to create a common public vernacular available to all citizens on an equal basis, not to tell them what they could or could not do in their own homes.

## America would become balkanized without English.

We don't have to imagine what a United States without a single universally understood and recognized language would be like. Examples of such balkanized communities are developing today, and none of them are very comforting for advocates of national unity.

California provides perhaps the most important test case. In his 2003 book, *Mexifornia: A State of Becoming*, historian and longtime California resident Victor David Hanson argues that the relaxation of English language use by the government has discouraged new immigrants from learning the language, with disastrous consequences for the common public culture of the state:

> Instead of meeting the challenge of turning immigrants into Americans, our teachers, politicians, and government officials for some time have taken the easier route of allowing a separatist culture. . . . The result is that we are seeing in the area the emergence of truly apartheid communities that resemble Mexican rather than American societies, and that are plagued by dismal schools, scant capital, many of the same social problems as Mexico, and a general neglect by the larger culture.

Hanson does not blame Spanish-speaking immigrants themselves: They are simply reacting to poor decisions made by the state authorities. All Californians suffer as a result. "A multiracial society works," Hanson insisted in an interview. "But a multicultural one—whose separatist identity transcends the enriching and diverse elements of food, fashion, entertainment, music, etc.—whether in Rwanda or the Balkans—does not, especially when new arrivals do not learn English."[12] Without a clear acknowledgement of the need for a common vernacular, might all America go the way of Hanson's Mexifornia?

## Summary

French political philosopher Alexis de Tocqueville once wrote how "language is perhaps the strongest, perhaps most enduring link which unites men."[13] As Tocqueville, a keen observer of early American society, knew well, English has been a common binding thread that has united Americans throughout the country's history; the economic, cultural, and political benefit of maintaining such a link among all citizens, no matter where in the world they originated, is clear. By abandoning the requirement for new Americans to learn English, we relegate those immigrants and their children to permanent second-class status. Moreover, we damage the brittle web of ties and associations that make our nation strong and indivisible. Making English the official language of the United States would not disadvantage immigrants whose native tongue is Spanish, Chinese, or any other vernaculars used around the world; it would empower them. It would not impede the growth of healthy cultural diversity; it would encourage it. If "E Pluribus Unum"—"Out of Many, One"—is to be more than a hollow motto, we need a national reference point that can only be found in a single language. The Klingons, should they ever arrive, will understand.

# It Is Unnecessary to Have an Official Language

My family immigrated to the United States four years ago. We were very happy but at the same time we were at a loss because we did not speak English. . . . I will never forget the first terrifying day at school. I remembered hearing my name said (which was not like the name my parents gave me), then the students laughed. I felt so ashamed and ridiculed. . . . My years at the junior high were very sad and lonely. I did not learn much English. My unpliable tongue could not pronounce some English sounds such as "th" and my accent was so thick that no one could understand. I could not do what other students did. I thought of myself as useless.

So recalled Thuy Tien Pham, a high school student from Morgan City, Louisiana, in a national writing competition in 2000. Originally from Vietnam, Thuy struggled throughout her early years in the American education system, in which she was instructed only in English. The breakthrough for her came when she transferred to a school with a bilingual program. "I can now take a hopeful look beyond the narrow horizon of our present life. I continue to preserve my language and culture through my letters to my grandmother, and to perfect my English by reading lots of literature in English. My ultimate goal will be to become a bilingual teacher. . . . I feel privileged and blessed with a 'bilingual brain.' I AM PROUD OF IT."[1]

Experiences such as Thuy's are common for young immigrants arriving in the United States. Solid research has shown again and again that a bilingual approach to educating students who have little or no prior background in English is the best means of improving their test scores in all subjects, including English. Bilingualism has been under severe attack from a powerful "English-only" lobby for some years now. In 1998, California—the state with the largest number of non–native English speakers in its education system—saw the approval of Proposition 227, a ballot initiative that effectively ended most bilingual education in the state's public schools. The great majority of California students classified as "English Language Learners" (ELLs) suddenly found themselves in English-only classrooms, a sink-or-swim approach to language education that, as Thuy's case shows, can fail individual students badly.

This is the problem with all English-only proposals, whether they are related to education or to public administration: They might be advocated with the best intentions, but their one-size-fits-all approach to language is arbitrary and unjust. Nobody would quarrel with the idea that immigrants need to learn English. Indeed, a basic competency in English is a requirement of the U.S. citizenship exam, a fact conveniently forgotten by those pushing for Official English laws.

Just as it would be unrealistic to expect most Americans to travel abroad and immediately understand the foreign languages they encounter, so non-English-speaking immigrants need time to develop their linguistic skills. Some people, particularly those of older generations, pick up languages more slowly than others do. Are their civil liberties to be placed under suspension until they have reached a satisfactory level of English comprehension? There is nothing in the Constitution about placing citizens in a hierarchy of rights and privileges according to national origin. Official English laws are not only unnecessary, their application of capricious inequality makes them un-American.

### America has always been a multilingual nation.

Since America declared its independence in 1776, the majority of citizens have spoken English as their first language. What about the minority of Americans who speak little or no English? Have their numbers markedly increased in the past couple of decades, as proponents of Official English laws claim? Are we facing an unprecedented wave of immigrants who cannot understand English or refuse to learn it?

Hardly. In many respects the United States is *less* multilingual today than it was a century ago. It is true that the number of languages spoken throughout the United States has steadily increased, as the range of countries from which immigrants derive has broadened. The percentage of non–English speakers in modern America, however, has dwindled overall. In 1890, there were four and a half times as many residents who could speak no English than there were 100 years later. At the dawn of the twentieth century, large areas of the United States, such as French-speaking Louisiana and the German-speaking Midwest, had sizable foreign-language communities that supported their own newspaper and publishing industries. Far from being a homogeneous mass of English speakers, the Americans of the Gilded Age were even more divided by language than we are today. So much for the good old days!

What *has* remained constant is the complaint that immigrants are not assimilating fast enough into English-speaking society. In 1911, an immigration commission sponsored by the federal government alleged that Jews, Italians, and Eastern Europeans were not learning English as quickly as previous generations of immigrants, such as the Germans and Scandinavians, had. These "revelations" were fueled more by anti-immigrant prejudice than by sound research; complaining about poor language skills was a way of tarnishing the newcomers as "un-American," perpetual strangers who were either unable or unwilling to assimilate into American society. As we now know, this allegation was ground-less. Immigrants from Sicily, Poland, and Russia became just as good American citizens as any other groups of people. There is no reason to believe that today's immigrants from Mexico, Korea, India, and Senegal will, in the long run, fare any differently.[2]

The idea that English is under threat in this country also has a long heritage. There is a popular folk belief that German would have become the official language of the United States in 1795 if not for a single politician in the House of Representatives. No such proposal was ever made, and the story seems to spring from a confusion of several unrelated anecdotes. In fact, most of the Founding Fathers believed that their new government should steer clear of official languages. When John Adams proposed the creation of an academy to dictate the use of English across the country, his idea was rejected as inconsistent with the principles of American liberty.[3]

## The costs of multilingual government and education are exaggerated.

One of the arguments made by supporters of Proposition 227 in California was that the cost of bilingual education was drain-ing the state's school system of badly needed resources. Actually, the "waste" of bilingualism has been blown out of proportion. True, teaching students with limited English proficiency is more expensive than the education of fluent English speakers, but that is true no matter what the language of instruction happens to be. A comparison between English-only and bilingual education of ELL students made by the California Legislature found that the cost per student in both cases varied little.[4] In fact, bilingualism saves money by producing students who are better educated and better equipped to enter America's job market.

The argument that the U.S. government will have to spend billions of dollars producing forms and information booklets in every language under the sun is another false charge levied by the Official English lobby. First, hardly any federal documents need to be produced in anything but English, and that situation seems

## The "German Vote" Urban Legend

Legend has it that in 1795 a bill to establish German as the official language of the fledgling United States of America was defeated in Congress by a single vote. There never was such a vote; indeed, there wasn't any such bill, either. A proposal before Congress in 1795 merely recommended the printing of federal laws in German as well as English, and no bill was ever actually voted upon.

This most famous of language legends began when a group of German-Americans from Augusta, Virginia, petitioned Congress, and in response to their petition a House committee recommended publishing three thousand sets of laws in German and distributing them to the states (with copies of statutes printed in English as well). The House debated this proposal on 13 January 1795 without reaching a decision, and a vote to adjourn and consider the recommendation at a later date was defeated by one vote, 42 to 41. There was no vote on an actual bill, merely a vote on whether or not to adjourn. Because the motion to adjourn did not pass, the matter was dropped. It was from this roll call on adjournment that the "German missed becoming the official language of the USA by one vote" legend sprang.

The House debated translating federal statutes into German again on 16 February 1795, but the final result was the approval of a bill to publish existing and future federal statutes in English only. This bill was approved by the Senate as well and signed into law by President George Washington a month later. The legend lives on, though, presented as a vivid lesson that the foundations of our world aren't always as solid as we think.

Source: "The German Vote," Urban Legends Reference Pages. http://www.snopes.com/language/apocryph/german.htm

unlikely to change regardless of the law. Between 1990 and 1994, the U.S. General Accounting Office, which was asked to audit the Government Printing Office's production of foreign language material, found only 265 examples out of 400,000 titles; 99.94 percent of all documents were in English exclusively. This was exactly the period in which critics were complaining about a tidal wave of translation! Second, the few government documents that *are* available in languages other than English tend to be created on grounds of cost-effectiveness. The IRS, for example, finds that it makes financial sense to provide tax information in Spanish; that way, Spanish speakers have no excuse for not filing their 1040s in a timely and accurate way. A federal law mandating that all federal materials have to be written in English would likely cost more than it saved and create great inconvenience for the government as well as citizens. In 1996, the Justice Department urged senators not to pass such a bill, arguing that vital aspects of their law enforcement work would be made needlessly complex and costly as a result. [5]

## An official English policy would hurt immigrants.

There is something deeply ironic in the claim that English is under threat in the United States today. The rise of English as the world's primary language of communication has been one of the most remarkable stories of the past 50 years. Around the globe, millions of men, women, and children daily are acquiring the English skills that they believe are essential to their economic and social fortunes. It is difficult to take the idea that English is about to disappear seriously when more people than ever—throughout the world—are speaking it!

In the United States, the majority of non–English speakers rapidly pick up the language. Indeed, linguistic assimilation today happens much faster than it did with earlier generations of immigrants from Southern and Eastern Europe. Research has shown that 19 out of every 20 first-generation Mexican Americans are proficient in English, that 90 percent of Latinos older than 5 speak English in their households, and that, among second-generation immigrants from Mexico—people whose parents originally came from outside the United States—half have stopped speaking Spanish entirely.[6] All this is taking place without any Official English laws. No wonder that one university professor, when asked about the need to make English the official language of the country, said that it "seems like passing a law to declare that air or oxygen is the official respiratory gas."[7]

An Official English law may not, in the long run, have much effect one way or another on Americans' ability to speak the language, but, in the short term, it *will* cause great disadvantages to first-generation immigrants. People cannot acquire language skills overnight. Their day-to-day economic, medical, and civic needs cannot be placed in furlough while they sit in English-immersion classes. Immigrants need to be able to understand basic public information, use health services, and take part in the labor force. They have the right and responsibility to be active members of the community, following current events in their neighborhoods and nationwide and voting. For this reason, many people believe that the Fourteenth Amendment, which requires the federal government to apply equal protection under the law to all citizens, would make any attempt to apply an English-only law unconstitutional. Because the Supreme Court has yet to rule on this issue, the question remains unanswered for now. Clearly there is something deeply inequitable about denying immigrants the opportunity to enjoy basic rights on account of their place of origin.

## Linguistic intolerance will hurt American society.

Perhaps the biggest problem with an Official English law is the message that it would send out through wider American culture. Advocates of the idea are careful to say they are only proposing restrictions on *government* use of foreign languages; people would be free to conduct their business in any vernacular they choose in private life. Strictly speaking, this is correct, but it ignores the slippery-slope effect that such a law would have. Its initial scope might be restricted to public matters. Once a climate of linguistic intolerance is created, however, it can easily expand to include other realms of life.

There are practical examples of this in the United States today: Across the country, cities have passed ordinances that make it unlawful to use languages other than English on privately owned commercial signs. Proposals to prohibit Spanish-language radio stations and to prevent telephone companies from hiring bilingual staff or printing non-English directories have been made.[8]

## Problem or Resource?

Monolinguals cherish a number of myths about how a second language is acquired. On the one hand, the task seems terribly onerous. Americans who struggled to learn a foreign language in school recall the drudgery of memorizing vocabulary and grammar, not to mention the embarrassment of attempting actual communication. (Woe unto those who tried to use their high school French in Quebec!) As adults with little to show for the experience, they tend to despair of the whole idea of language learning. On the other hand, children make it look so effortless. They seem to "pick up" a strange tongue within a few weeks, chattering away with new playmates before their parents can utter a respectable sentence.

Although these perceptions reflect real phenomena, they are distorted by social prejudices. Many Americans conclude, for example, that the most effective way to learn a second language is to be "totally immersed" in it. Necessity seems the best motivator. Conversely, the option of relying on one's mother tongue appears to weaken the incentive to learn another. This immersion fetish—the idea that maximum exposure and maximum will are what count in language acquisition—inspires much of the skepticism surrounding bilingual education. According to this reasoning, if children are allowed to keep their life-preservers, they will never swim unassisted.

"I got the total immersion method," claims Mark LaPorta, chairman of the Florida English Campaign. A second-generation American, he grew up speaking English, although "a big chunk of my people spoke Italian as the primary

The success of these programs is spotty. An English-only ordinance in Farmers Branch, Texas, was made unenforceable by a court, while towns in New Jersey and Missouri were forced to repeal their English-only laws because of political pressure.[9]

Private companies have tried to implement English-only rules on work premises and have disciplined employees for breaking these restrictions. Such rules are of questionable legality, and employees have had some success in fighting them in the courtroom. In 2001, the University of the Incarnate Word in San Antonio, Texas, settled a lawsuit over English-only policies for

---

language. My father would rather have a conversation in Italian than in English." To uphold the tradition, LaPorta was sent to learn Italian from relatives in the old country. "My father put me on an airplane for southern Italy when I was five and my brother was four, kissed us on the forehead, and said, 'Speak or don't eat.' For thirty to forty days, there was no English, and we ate fine. My family on that side were all schoolteachers. We didn't have to sit down for an hour and make a class out of it. But I was dumped in and I learned good Italian."

LaPorta is fortunate for the experience. Today, in contrast to most Euro-ethnics, he can communicate freely with his elders in their favored language. What child would not benefit from a similar opportunity? Yet he is mistaken to generalize lessons for non-English-speaking children in American schools. Too often, their experience is to be "dumped" into a strange environment, without relatives who can help them, and expected to use a poorly grasped language in learning to read and other challenging pursuits. Intimidation and confusion are hardly ideal conditions for acquiring English. Furthermore, the stakes are considerably higher. For minority students, falling behind means being labeled a slow learner (perhaps even "learning disabled"), and it greatly increases their likelihood of dropping out. Life chances can hinge on school performance at an early age.

Source: "Problem or Resource?" excerpted from *Hold Your Tongue: Bilingualism and the Politics of English-Only*, by James Crawford (1992). http://ourworld.compuserve.com/homepages/JWCRAWFORD/HYT.htm

$2.4 million. The settlement was reached by the Equal Employment Opportunity Commission on behalf of 18 Hispanic custodians, some of whom knew how to speak only Spanish. Ida Castro, chairwoman for the EEOC, said, "As employers face the challenge of a rapidly changing workforce, they will serve themselves well by creating work environments that are conducive to diversity and putting strategies in place to ease racial and ethnic tensions."[10]

Forbidding government use of any vernacular other than English tells Americans, in effect, that there is something second-rate or suspect—something un-American—about speaking another language. As this message spreads into the larger community, it encourages further discriminatory policies toward non–English speakers. Immigrants already face enough hostility and intolerance; do we really need to add to their burdens by creating new rules to disadvantage and discredit them?

## Summary

About half of the countries in the world have one or more official languages. In many of these countries, particularly those that have little tradition of foreign immigration—countries that do not much resemble the United States—this works perfectly well. In others, however, arguments about the status of language have created domestic tension: Belgium, which is divided into Flemish- and French-speaking districts, is notorious for the internal conflict that language law has created. In Turkey, the government has been accused of using its official language as a weapon with which to punish and harass ethnic minorities such as the Kurds. French-speaking Quebec, which almost broke apart from the rest of Canada in the 1990s because of ethno-cultural rifts, is a prime example of the folly of trying to legislate language. Many of the province's problems have arisen from the government's clumsy attempts to enforce what citizens may or may not say in public and in their workplaces.

The fact is that the United States works best when the state interferes as little as possible in matters that do not concern it. Language is a prime example. The majority of people in America will continue to use English as their primary language without any prodding from Washington. The majority of immigrants will quickly learn and speak English, too. For the relatively small number of people who cannot function in an English environment, however, some commonsense concessions need to be made. An English-only law would cause far more problems than it would ever solve. English is the most powerful form of communication in the world; it doesn't need a government bodyguard to look after it.

# The Future of Immigration Policy

T he previous chapters introduced the key facts and concepts of American immigration policy and discussed four of the most contentious issues involving immigrants today. This conclusion examines some of the latest developments in the public immigration debate, developments that will likely influence the policies of the next president of the United States.

## The 2004 "Guest Worker" Proposals

One of the less dramatic, but nonetheless important, consequences of the 9/11 attacks on the United States was that President Bush had to postpone the U.S.-Mexico immigration and frontier-control initiative that he had been working on with Mexico's then-president, Vicente Fox. As a former governor of Texas and someone familiar with the problems of illegal immigration into his border state, President Bush placed a high priority on reaching some kind of mutually acceptable agreement with Mexico. The terrorist attacks pushed the issue to the sidelines, and the public's mood was far less sympathetic toward immigrants in general in the wake of al-Qaeda's atrocities. It wasn't until early 2004 that President Bush was able to revisit the idea of creating a "guest worker" program to try to tackle illegal immigration.[1]

A guest worker is not a permanently legalized immigrant but an alien who is allowed to live and work in the country for a fixed number of years. Employees and students who are in the United States on an H- or J-type nonimmigrant visa are examples of guest workers. President Bush's proposal, announced in January 2004, was to create a category of guest-worker status specifically targeted at the millions of people living in the United States as illegal immigrants. People who received the new visa would be permitted to stay in the country and work for up to three years, after which they would have to have their papers renewed, and they would need to be employed or have the promise of a job on the way at the time they became guest workers. If they broke the law or otherwise ran afoul of the authorities, their right to remain in the United States would be revoked. President Bush argued that this is the only practical way to bring the country's illegal-immigrant population out of the criminal shadows and at the same time ensure a smooth flow of labor for America's businesses. While President Bush reiterated his support for a guest worker program in his 2008 State of the Union address, it seems unlikely that such a program will be enacted before the end of his term in January 2009.

The politics of the guest-worker program are quite complex, however. On one hand, the Mexican-American and wider Latino vote has become increasingly important in presidential elections—witness the key role that Florida, which has a large Hispanic population, played in the 2000 election. During the 2008 election, Republican Senator John McCain and Democratic Senator Barack Obama needed to address the immigration issue. Because of his support for Bush's guest-worker proposal, McCain had to confront the many conservative Republicans who opposed the president's proposal, arguing that

## Remarks by President George W. Bush on Immigration Policy, January 2004

As a nation that values immigration, and depends on immigration, we should have immigration laws that work and make us proud. Yet today we do not. Instead, we see many employers turning to the illegal labor market. We see millions of hard-working men and women condemned to fear and insecurity in a massive, undocumented economy. Illegal entry across our borders makes more difficult the urgent task of securing the homeland. The system is not working. Our nation needs an immigration system that serves the American economy, and reflects the American Dream....

I propose a new temporary worker program that will match willing foreign workers with willing American employers, when no Americans can be found to fill the jobs. This program will offer legal status, as temporary workers, to the millions of undocumented men and women now employed in the United States, and to those in foreign countries who seek to participate in the program and have been offered employment here. This new system should be clear and efficient, so employers are able to find workers quickly and simply.

All who participate in the temporary worker program must have a job, or, if not living in the United States, a job offer. The legal status granted by this program will last three years and will be renewable—but it will have an end. Participants who do not remain employed, who do not follow the rules of the program, or who break the law will not be eligible for continued participation and will be required to return to their home.

...The temporary worker program I am proposing today represents the best tradition of our society, a society that honors the law, and welcomes the newcomer. This plan will help return order and fairness to our immigration system, and in so doing we will honor our values, by showing our respect for those who work hard and share in the ideals of America.

Source: "President Bush Proposes New Temporary Worker Program." http://www.whitehouse.gov/news/releases/2004/01/20040107-3.html

it is in effect amnesty for illegal immigrants, rewarding them for criminal behavior. Obama supported immigration reform, voting for bills that provide guest workers a path toward citizenship and more funding for immigrant social services, but opposed providing amnesty for illegal immigrants already in the country. This stance required Obama to assuage concerns on both ends of the spectrum that he is neither an open-border liberal nor a pro-business shell man who is not protecting illegal immigrants from capricious employers.

## Asylum Seekers and Refugees

The standard means of acquiring permanent residency in the United States are through work or family connections. There is a third possibility: asylum or refugee status. The definition of what constitutes an asylum seeker or a refugee is taken from the 1967 United Nations Convention and Protocol Relating to the Status of Refugees, which describes them as:

> Any person who is outside any country of such person's nationality or, in the case of a person having no nationality, is outside any country in which such person last habitually resided, and who is unwilling or unable to return to . . . that country because of persecution or a well-founded fear of persecution on account of race, religion, nationality, membership in a particular social group, or political opinion.[2]

Asylum seekers are physically present in the United States (sometimes illegally) at the time they make their petition to the government; refugees are outside the United States. Otherwise, there is no real distinction between the two groups.

This apparently simple definition has been complicated by the demands of politics. In principle, all potential refugees or asylum seekers are treated equally by U.S. authorities and are subject to the same quotas on the number of refugees who can be permitted to enter the country in any given year, but in practice

Congress has historically interfered in the process by creating special conditions for certain groups. The 1966 Cuban Adjustment Act (public law 89-732) was amended in 1995 so that just about any Cuban citizen who manages to reach American shores is automatically granted refugee status regardless of quotas. (Cubans who are intercepted by the Coast Guard en route are sent back.) This means that if they remain in the United States for one year, they are allowed to petition for permanent residence and later for U.S. citizenship. During the Cold War, other exceptions were made for Communist countries. As Democratic lawmaker Eugene McCarthy noted, "Decisions about refugee status . . . in the United States are shaped by a variety of sources: foreign governments, the media, political pressure groups, and the people who claim to be refugees. Considerations have gone well beyond the simple desire of the American people to assist those who are truly persecuted."[3]

There is also the problem of defining what "persecution" is. In many cases, such as ethnic communities that have been victims of racial violence or dissident writers and journalists who have been targeted by dictatorial regimes, the meaning is straightforward enough. What of, say, the much knottier problem of abortion? In 1996, Congress expanded the definition of persecution to include people who have been subject to strict family-planning controls, such as the "one child per family" rule that operates in China. This created the potential for massive waves of refugees, and some critics of immigration policy complained that it opened up opportunities for "economic refugees," people who are not sincerely looking to escape persecution but who wish to immigrate to the United States to seek work and who are willing to exploit loopholes in the law to do it. At the moment, asylum admissions to the United States are down a little (about 100,000 per year) from the peak years of the early 1990s, when another 20,000 or so people were admitted annually, and refugees represent a relatively small

The United States accepts a set number of immigrants each year because of their status as asylum seekers and refugees, or because they would face torture or persecution in their home countries. Above, the family of José Arturo Medrano gathers around his photograph. Their request to stay in the United States was bolstered after Medrano was murdered months after his deportation to his native El Salvador.

proportion of the total number of incoming foreign residents. The potential for a large future increase is there, however, especially given the political instability of nearby countries such as Haiti. Will the United States have to redefine the way that it treats refugees if their numbers expand in the early twenty-first century?

### Immigrant Tracking

In the investigation into the 9/11 attacks, one of the most worrying discoveries was that all the airplane hijackers had been able

## Barack Obama Addresses The Immigration Issue During The 2008 Presidential Campaign

Many pundits were surprised that immigration did not materialize as a major issue in the 2008 presidential campaign. In Barack Obama's campaign material, one gets some indication of how his presidential administration will handle immigration issues in the future.

### Plan for Immigration

"The time to fix our broken immigration system is now ... We need stronger enforcement on the border and at the workplace ... But for reform to work, we also must respond to what pulls people to America ... Where we can reunite families, we should. Where we can bring in more foreign-born workers with the skills our economy needs, we should."
—*Barack Obama, Statement on U.S. Senate Floor, May 23, 2007*

### THE PROBLEM

**Undocumented population is exploding:** The number of undocumented immigrants in the country has increased more than 40 percent since 2000. Every year, more than a half-million people come illegally or illegally overstay their visas.

**Immigration bureaucracy is broken:** The immigration bureaucracy is broken and overwhelmed, forcing legal immigrants to wait years for applications.

**Immigration raids are ineffective:** Despite a sevenfold increase in recent years, immigration raids only netted 3,600 arrests in 2006 and have placed all the burdens of a broken system onto immigrant families.

### BARACK OBAMA'S PLAN

#### Create Secure Borders

Obama wants to preserve the integrity of our borders. He supports additional personnel, infrastructure, and technology on the border and at our ports of entry.

to illegally obtain Social Security cards and state-issued driver's licenses despite having entered the United States only on non-immigrant visas. Indeed, one of the repercussions of 9/11 was a

### Improve Our Immigration System

Obama believes we must fix the dysfunctional immigration bureaucracy and increase the number of legal immigrants to keep families together and meet the demand for jobs that employers cannot fill.

### Remove Incentives to Enter Illegally

Obama will remove incentives to enter the country illegally by cracking down on employers who hire undocumented immigrants.

### Bring People Out of the Shadows

Obama supports a system that allows undocumented immigrants who are in good standing to pay a fine, learn English, and go to the back of the line for the opportunity to become citizens.

### Work with Mexico

Obama believes we need to do more to promote economic development in Mexico to decrease illegal immigration.

### BARACK OBAMA'S RECORD

- **Crack Down on Employers:** Obama championed a proposal to create a system so employers can verify that their employees are legally eligible to work in the U.S.

- **Fix the Bureaucracy:** Obama joined Rep. Luis Gutierrez (D-IL) to introduce the Citizenship Promotion Act to ensure that immigration application fees are both reasonable and fair. Obama also introduced legislation that passed the Senate to improve the speed and accuracy of FBI background checks.

- **Respect Families:** Obama introduced amendments to put greater emphasis on keeping immigrant families together.

Excepted from Barack Obama for President Web site, accessed June 2, 2008. http://www.barackobama.com/issues/immigration/

major shake-up of the American immigration system, including the dissolution of the old INS and the creation of the new bureaus described in the Introduction. It had become increasingly obvious that there was no effective tracking system for resident and non-resident aliens in the United States. Once inside the Customs or border frontier, aliens were able to basically disappear from sight of the government—in order to illicitly live and work or for more sinister reasons such as terrorism—and the market for forged or criminally obtained documents was vast and expanding.

In response to this perceived failure, the federal government announced the creation of a comprehensive tracking system for residents who originated from "high-risk" nations, mainly in the Middle East. Known as the National Security Entry-Exit Registration System, or NSEERS, this required all men older than 16 who were living in the United States but still citizens of the targeted countries to register with an immigration office or face arrest or deportation. NSEERS, which went into effect in fall 2002, involved tens of thousands of registrations and was heavily criticized for being discriminatory and deliberately confusing—for example, by changing important deadlines without properly advertising the fact. "NSEERS is a poorly implemented plan that has failed to advance our national security or improve efficiency within our immigration system," said a representative of the American Civil Liberties Union. "The failure to publicize the new deadlines appears to be a continuation of the pattern of selectively arresting, detaining and deporting Middle Eastern and Muslim men in the United States."[4] Faced with these complaints, the Homeland Security Department suspended some of the provisions of NSEERS in 2003, but introduced a parallel program called US-VISIT (U.S. Visitor and Immigrant Status Indicator Technology) that required many nonimmigrants traveling into or through the United States to provide fingerprints and have a digital photograph taken.

Schemes such as NSEERS and US-VISIT are controversial because they intersect with two powerful themes in United

States culture: the natural desire to defend the homeland against foreign threat and the quintessential American love of privacy. We consider the threat from terrorism very real, but we also cherish the liberty to keep our private behavior out of the eyes of government. That is why a plan to register and record information about residents—even noncitizens—goes so much against the grain. The problem, ultimately, is weighing two important but contradictory aims: security and confidentiality. It also shows how immigration issues have repercussions that extend to the lives of native-born citizens, too.

One thing about immigration can be said with some authority: It is a subject—either a problem or an opportunity—that is not going away. Nearly all Americans, regardless of whether they have ancestors who traveled across the Atlantic on the *Mayflower*, are the products of immigration, and they will continue to grapple with its complexities throughout the upcoming century. Even if no final agreement on the desirability or danger of the system is reached (and history suggests that one thing Americans are very good at is failing to agree), we all at least need to accept that the questions it raises are not simple ones and rarely if ever require clear-cut choices. Honesty and open-mindedness about immigration are essential responsibilities of *all* Americans.

# APPENDIX ⫘▷

## Beginning Legal Research

The goals of each book in the POINT/COUNTERPOINT series are not only to give the reader a basic introduction to a controversial issue affecting society, but also to encourage the reader to explore the issue more fully. This Appendix is meant to serve as a guide to the reader in researching the current state of the law as well as exploring some of the public policy arguments as to why existing laws should be changed or new laws are needed.

Although some sources of law can be found primarily in law libraries, legal research has become much faster and more accessible with the advent of the Internet. This Appendix discusses some of the best starting points for free access to laws and court decisions, but surfing the Web will uncover endless additional sources of information. Before you can research the law, however, you must have a basic understanding of the American legal system.

The most important source of law in the United States is the Constitution. Originally enacted in 1787, the Constitution outlines the structure of our federal government, as well as setting limits on the types of laws that the federal government and state governments can enact. Through the centuries, a number of amendments have added to or changed the Constitution, most notably the first 10 amendments, which collectively are known as the "Bill of Rights" and which guarantee important civil liberties.

Reading the plain text of the Constitution provides little information. For example, the Constitution prohibits "unreasonable searches and seizures" by the police. To understand concepts in the Constitution, it is necessary to look to the decisions of the U.S. Supreme Court, which has the ultimate authority in interpreting the meaning of the Constitution. For example, the U.S. Supreme Court's 2001 decision in *Kyllo v. United States* held that scanning the outside of a person's house using a heat sensor to determine whether the person is growing marijuana is an unreasonable search—if it is done without first getting a search warrant from a judge. Each state also has its own constitution and a supreme court that is the ultimate authority on its meaning.

Also important are the written laws, or "statutes," passed by the U.S. Congress and the individual state legislatures. As with constitutional provisions, the U.S. Supreme Court and the state supreme courts are the ultimate authorities in interpreting the meaning of federal and state laws, respectively. However, the U.S. Supreme Court might find that a state law violates the U.S. Constitution, and a state supreme court might find that a state law violates either the state or U.S. Constitution.

Not every controversy reaches either the U.S. Supreme Court or the state supreme courts, however. Therefore, the decisions of other courts are also important. Trial courts hear evidence from both sides and make a decision, while appeals courts review the decisions made by trial courts. Sometimes rulings from appeals courts are appealed further to the U.S. Supreme Court or the state supreme courts.

Lawyers and courts refer to statutes and court decisions through a formal system of citations. Use of these citations reveals which court made the decision or which legislature passed the statute, and allows one to quickly locate the statute or court case online or in a law library. For example, the Supreme Court case *Brown v. Board of Education* has the legal citation 347 U.S. 483 (1954). At a law library, this 1954 decision can be found on page 483 of volume 347 of the U.S. Reports, which are the official collection of the Supreme Court's decisions. On the following page, you will find sample of all the major kinds of legal citation.

Finding sources of legal information on the Internet is relatively simple thanks to "portal" sites such as findlaw.com and lexisone.com, which allow the user to access a variety of constitutions, statutes, court opinions, law review articles, news articles, and other useful sources of information. For example, findlaw.com offers access to all Supreme Court decisions since 1893. Other useful sources of information include gpo.gov, which contains a complete copy of the U.S. Code, and thomas.loc.gov, which offers access to bills pending before Congress, as well as recently passed laws. Of course, the Internet changes every second of every day, so it is best to do some independent searching.

Of course, many people still do their research at law libraries, some of which are open to the public. For example, some state governments and universities offer the public access to their law collections. Law librarians can be of great assistance, as even experienced attorneys need help with legal research from time to time.

## Common Citation Forms

| Source of Law | Sample Citation | Notes |
|---|---|---|
| U.S. Supreme Court | *Employment Division v. Smith*, 485 U.S. 660 (1988) | The U.S. Reports is the official record of Supreme Court decisions. There is also an unofficial Supreme Court ("S. Ct.") reporter. |
| U.S. Court of Appeals | *United States v. Lambert*, 695 F.2d 536 (11th Cir. 1983) | Appellate cases appear in the Federal Reporter, designated by "F." The 11th Circuit has jurisdiction in Alabama, Florida, and Georgia. |
| U.S. District Court | *Carillon Importers, Ltd. v. Frank Pesce Group, Inc.*, 913 F.Supp. 1559 (S.D.Fla. 1996) | Federal trial-level decisions are reported in the Federal Supplement ("F. Supp."). Some states have multiple federal districts; this case originated in the Southern District of Florida. |
| U.S. Code | Thomas Jefferson Commemoration Commission Act, 36 U.S.C., §149 (2002) | Sometimes the popular names of legislation—names with which the public may be familiar—are included with the U.S. Code citation. |
| State Supreme Court | *Sterling v. Cupp*, 290 Ore. 611, 614, 625 P.2d 123, 126 (1981) | The Oregon Supreme Court decision is reported in both the state's reporter and the Pacific regional reporter. |
| State Statute | Pennsylvania Abortion Control Act of 1982, 18 Pa. Cons. Stat. 3203-3220 (1990) | States use many different citation formats for their statutes. |

## Cases and Legislation

**1882 Immigration Act**
First general immigration law instituted by the U.S. government. The act introduced an immigration tax and restricted the immigration of certain groups, including convicts and those unable to care for themselves.

**Chinese Exclusion Act**
Also passed in 1882, banned entrance of Chinese laborers on the premise that they threatened the "good order" of certain areas.

**Immigration and Nationality Act of 1952**
This bill codified previous immigration acts and laws, established new quotas and allowed certain immigrants, including spouses and children of American citizens, to enter free from quota restrictions. Also set disqualifying factors for immigration that included disease, poverty, and illiteracy.

**Immigration and Nationality Act Amendment, 1965**
Eliminated national origins quota systems and filled general quota by choosing immigrants with certain personal attributes. The amendment reserved the majority of the quota for family members of American citizens and dictated that the remaining immigrants admitted must be escaping persecution or possessing desirable education, ability, or experience.

**Immigration Reform and Control Act of 1986**
This act was passed to control illegal immigration to the United States through employee sanctions, increased funding for enforcement, and amnesty provisions.

**Proposition 187**
Proposition introduced in California in 1994 to deny illegal immigrants social services, public education, and health care.

**Proposition 227**
California ballot proposition, approved in 1998, which ended most bilingual education in California public schools.

**Executive Order 13166**
Decree signed by President Bill Clinton in 2000 which requires all federally funded institutions to provide services in any language requested.

## Terms and Concepts

| | |
|---|---|
| Alien | Dual nationality |
| Amnesty | Green card |
| Asylum | Guest worker |
| Balkanize | Nativist |
| *Coyote* | Refugee |

## Introduction: A Scene From American Life

1 Oath of Allegiance, http://www.uscis.gov/
propub/ProPubVAP.jsp?dockey=6d82936
6567c8d453799c25eb504028b
2 Based on Tom Mashberg, "New Americans Enjoy Rewards of Citizenship,"
*Boston Herald*, April 17, 2003.
3 Quoted in "Overview of INS History,"
http://uscis.gov/graphics/aboutus/
history/articles/OVIEW.htm
4 1882 Chinese Exclusion Act. http://
www-marine.stanford.edu/chinese.htm
5 Professor Stanley Renshon, quoted in
Siobhan McDonough, "Mixed Messages
Common to Government," Associated
Press, May 23, 2003.
6 Steven A. Camarota, "Immigrants in the
United States, 2007: A Profile of America's Foreign-Born Population," Center
for Immigration Studies, http://www.cis.
org/articles/2007/back1007.pdf
7 Department of Homeland Security,
"Annual Flow Report: Temporary
Admissions of Nonimmigrants to the
United States: 2006," July 2007. http://
www.dhs.gov/xlibrary/assets/statistics/
publications/NI_FR_2006_508_final.pdf
8 Ibid.
9 Office of Immigration Statistics, "Annual
Flow Report: U.S. Legal Permanent Residents: 2007," March 2008. http://www.
dhs.gov/xlibrary/assets/statistics/
publications/LPR_FR_2007.pdf
10 "Persons Naturalized by Gender, Age,
Marital Status, and Occupation," *2006
Yearbook of Immigration Statistics,*Table
24, p. 59. http://www.dhs.gov/xlibrary/
assets/statistics/yearbook/2006/OIS_
2006_Yearbook.pdf
11 "Deportable Aliens Located: Fiscal Years
1925 to 2006", *2006 Yearbook of Immigration Statistics,* Table 34, p. 91.
http://www.dhs.gov/xlibrary/assets/
statistics/yearbook/2006/OIS_2006_
Yearbook.pdf Illegal alien estimate
from the Department of Homeland
Security report "Estimates of the
Unauthorized Immigrant Population
Residing in the United States: January
2006," August 2007. http://www.dhs.
gov/xlibrary/assets/statistics/
publications/ill_pe_2006.pdf

## Point: The United States Should Crack Down Harder on Illegal Immigrants

1 Ginger Thompson, "Crossing with
Strangers: Children at the Border; Littlest
Immigrants, Left in the Hands of Smugglers," *New York Times,* November 3,
2003.
2 U.S. Department of Health and Human
Services, Administration for Children &
Families, Office of Refugee Resettlement.
http://www.acf.hhs.gov/programs/orr/
programs/unaccompanied_alien_
children.htm
3 All quotations from Ginger Thompson,
"Littlest Immigrants, Left in Hands of
Smugglers."
4 Department of Homeland Security
report, "Estimates of the Unauthorized
Immigrant Population Residing in the
United States: January 2006," August
2007. http://www.dhs.gov/xlibrary/assets/
statistics/publications/ill_pe_2006.pdf
Federation for American Immigration Reform, "How Many Illegal
Aliens?" http://www.fairus.org/site/
PageServer?pagename=iic_
immigrationissuecentersb8ca
5 Migration Policy Institute, "Unauthorized Immigration to the United States"
fact sheet. http://www.migrationpolicy.
org/pubs/USImmigrationFacts2003.pdf
6 Federation for American Immigration Reform, "What's Wrong With
Illegal Immigration?" fact sheet, March
2005. http://www.fairus.org/site/
PageServer?pagename=iic_
immigrationissuecenters7443
7 Polly Gonzalez, "Illegal Aliens Face
Exploitation in Valley," KLAS-TV,
May 8, 2003.
8 Federation for American Immigration
Reform, "The Cost of Illegal Immigration to Californians," November 2004.
http://www.fairus.org/site/DocServer/
ca_costs.pdf?docID=141
9 Federation for American Immigration
Reform, "FYI . . . New Illegal Immigration Statistics," May 2003. http://www.
fairus.org/site/PageServer?pagename=
research_researchf9b9
10 Federation for American Immigration
Reform, Jack Martin, "Breaking the

Piggy Bank: How Illegal Immigration Is Sending Schools into the Red," June 2005. http://www.fairus.org/site/PageServer?pagename=research_researchf6ad

11 Quoted in John Perazzo, "Illegal Immigration and Terrorism" FrontPageMazagine.com, December 18, 2002. http://www.frontpagemag.com/Articles/Printable.asp?ID=5147

12 Federation for American Immigration Reform, "Social Security Funds for Illegal Aliens?" November 2003. http://www.fairus.org/site/PageServer?pagename=iic_immigrationissuecenters3acf

13 "Wal-Mart Acknowledges US Immigration Probe," Agence France-Presse, November 4, 2003.

14 William J. Kole, "AP Finds E. Europeans Getting Illegal Jobs," Associated Press, October 31, 2003.

15 Center for Immigration Studies, "Illegal Immigration." http://www.cis.org/topics/illegalimmigration.html

16 Mark Krikorian, Center for Immigration Studies, "Fewer Immigrants, a Warmer Welcome: Fixing a Broken Immigration Policy," November 2003. http://www.cis.org/articles/2003/back1503.html

17 Center for Immigration Studies, "New INS Report: 1986 Amnesty Increased Illegal Immigration." http://www.cis.org/ articles/ 2000 /ins1986amnesty.html

**Counterpoint: The Key to Stopping Illegal Immigration Is to Reform the Law, Not to Punish People**

1 Lisa De Moraes, "ABC's Vision of Elian Interview Not '20/20,'" *Washington Post*, March 31, 2000.

2 Charles Krauthammer, quoted in "The Elian Debate," *PBS NewsHour*, April 26, 2000. http://www.pbs.org/newshour/bb/media/jan-june00/elian_4-26.html

3 Judy Mann, "Phony Defenders of Civil Liberties," *Washington Post*, April 28, 2000.

4 Nolo Martinez, "U.S. Must Take Closer Look at Illegal Immigrants," *Business Journal of the Greater Triad Area*, April

11, 2003. http://www.bizjournals.com/triad/stories/2003/04/14/editorial3.html

5 Kruti Dholakia, "The Problem of Illegal Immigrants: A Possible Policy Solution," November 2001. http://www.utdallas.edu/~kruti/problem_of_illegal_immigrants.pdf

6 Tim Wise, "Defending the Unwelcome Stranger," *LiP Magazine*, September 26, 2003. http://www.lipmagazine.org/articles/featwise_immigrationexcerpt.shtml

7 Ruben Castaneda, "Man Gets 6 Years for Enslaving Immigrant," *Washington Post*, August 15, 2000.

8 Geordie Greig, "Clinton writhes in Nannygate," *Sunday Times* (London), February 7, 1993.

9 Jeff Lustig and Dick Walker, "No Way Out: Immigrants and the New California," June 22, 1995. http://www-geography.berkeley.edu/projectsresources/CaliforniaStudies/pub_nowayout.htm

10 Niko Price, "U.S.-Mexico Border Crackdown Failing," Associated Press, November 2, 2003.

11 "Immigration: Time for Amnesty," *St. Louis Post-Dispatch*, October 20, 2003.

**Point: The United States Should Construct Physical Barriers on the Southern Border to Stem the Tide of Illegal Immigration**

1 Arthur H. Rotstein, "Anti-Illegal Immigration Group Gains National Foothold," Associated Press, December 17, 2005.

2 Border Fence Project, Accessed June 2, 2008. http://www.borderfenceproject.com/index.shtml

3 Ron Paul, Ron Paul for President Web site. Accessed June 2, 2008. http://www.ronpaul2008.com/issues/border-security-and-immigration-reform

4 Marta Tevares, "Fencing Out the Neighbors: Legal Implications of the U.S.-Mexico Border Security Fence," 14 Human Rights Br. 33 (Spring 2007). See *Chae Chan Ping v. United States*, 130 U.S. 581 (1889).

5 U.S. Constitution, Article I, Section 8.

6 Department of Homeland Security report "Estimates of the Unauthorized Immigrant Population Residing in the United States: January 2006," August 2007. http://www.dhs.gov/xlibrary/assets/statistics/publications/ill_pe_2006.pdf Federation for American Immigration Reform, "How Many Illegal Aliens?" updated October 2007. http://www.fairus.org/site/PageServer?pagename=iic_immigrationissuecentersb8ca

7 Tom A. Peter, "National Intelligence Estimate: Al Qaeda Stronger and a Threat to US Homeland," *Christian Science Monitor*, July 19, 2007.

8 House Committee on Homeland Security, "A Line in the Sand: Confronting the Threat at the Southwest Border," October 16, 2006. http://www.house.gov/mccaul/pdf/Investigaions-Border-Report.pdf

9 U.S. Drug Enforcement Administration, "Southwest Border Region Drug Transportation and Homeland Security Issues." Accessed June 2, 2008. http://www.usdoj.gov/dea/concern/18862/southwest_border.htm

10 Eileen Sullivan, "Its Future Uncertain, Barrier on the Border Going Up Quickly," Associated Press, April 28, 2008. http://www.foxnews.com/wires/2008Apr28/0,4670,OntheFence,00.html

11 Michael A. Fletcher and Jonathan Weisman, "Bush Signs Bill Authorizing 700-Mile Fence for Border," *Washington Post*, October 27, 2006, Page A04.

12 CBS Evening News, "Is The Costly Border Fence Worth It? U.S.-Mexico Fence Is Catching Fewer Illegal Immigrants, but Costing More," April 8, 2008. http://www.cbsnews.com/stories/2008/04/08/eveningnews/main4002554.shtml?source=related_story

13 Spencer S. Hsu, "Immigration Prosecutions Hit New High," *Washington Post*, June 2, 2008.

14 "Smuggling Tunnel Found Along Mexican Border," "Rita Cosby Specials," MSNBC.com, January 27, 2006. http://www.msnbc.msn.com/id/11060688

15 Department of Homeland Security, "More on the Border Fence," Updated April 23, 2008. http://www.

dhs.gov/xprevprot/programs/gc_1207842692831.shtm

16 Ibid.

17 Brenda Norrell, "Arizona Border Fence Environmental Impact Questioned," *Center for International Policy*, October 2, 2007. http://americas.irc-online.org/am/4599

18 Jerry Seper, "Chertoff Waives Rules on Fence; Completion of Border 'Enforcement Zone' Sought," *Washington Times*, September 15, 2005 Jim McElhatton, "Judge Rejects Greens' Bid to Halt Border Fence," *Washington Times*, December 20, 2007.

## Counterpoint: Physical Barriers on the U.S. Southern Border Will Not Solve Illegal Immigration Problems

1 BBC News, "Berlin Wall Timeline." Accessed June 2, 2008. http://news.bbc.co.uk/2/hi/europe/1484769.stm

2 BBC News, "Did David Hasselhoff Really Help End the Cold War?" Accessed June 2, 2008, http://news.bbc.co.uk/2/hi/uk_news/magazine/3465301.stm

3 Jacci Howard Bear, "The Fence-Cutters' War: Barbed Wire in Texas," About.com. Accessed June 2, 2008. http://austin.about.com/cs/history/a/barbed_wiretx_3.htm

4 Mark Stevenson, "Mexico Promises to Block Border Wall Plan," Associated Press, December 20, 2005. http://www.breitbart.com/article.php?id=D8EK9N0G6&show_article=1

5 News update from Web site of Representative Jose Serrano. Accessed June 2, 2008. http://www.house.gov/apps/list/speech/ny16_serrano/morenews/nl060317.html

6 Alex Cohen, "Border Fence Stirs Mixed Emotions," *NPR: Day to Day*, October 5, 2007. http://www.npr.org/templates/story/story.php?storyId=15034078

7 Jeanne Meserve, "Border Fence Dispute Brings Texas Showdown," CNN, January 17, 2008. http://www.cnn.com/2008/US/01/17/border.fence/index.html

8 CanadaInfo, "Canada and United States Border." Accessed June 2, 2008. http://www.craigmarlatt.com/canada/canada&the_world/canada&us_border.html

9  Janice Cheryl Beaver, "US International Borders: Brief Facts," *CRS Report for Congress*, Federation of American Scientists, November 9, 2006. http://www.fas.org/sgp/crs/misc/RS21729.pdf

10 CBS Evening News, "Is The Costly Border Fence Worth It? U.S.-Mexico Fence Is Catching Fewer Illegal Immigrants, But Costing More," April 8, 2008. http://www.cbsnews.com/stories/2008/04/08/eveningnews/main4002554.shtml?source=related_story

11 Ibid.

12 Sarah Anderson, "Immigration Solutions Lie Beyond Our Borders," Featured Views, CommonDreams.org, May, 25, 2006. http://www.commondreams.org/views06/0525-30.htm

13 "Border Fence Dispute Brings Texas Showdown," January 17, 2008.

14 Randal C. Archibold, "Border Fence Work Raises Environmental Concerns" *New York Times*, November 21, 2007. http://www.nytimes.com/2007/11/21/us/21fence.html?_r=1&oref=slogin

15 No Border Wall, "Environmental Impact." Accessed June 2, 2008. http://notexasborderwall.com/page4.htm

16 Ibid.

17 Ibid.

18 Ibid.

19 Manuel Roig-Franzia, "Mexico Calls U.S. Border Fence Severe Threat to Environment," *Washington Post*, November 16, 2007. http://www.washingtonpost.com/wp-dyn/content/article/2007/11/15/AR2007111502272.html

20 Juan Gonzalez, "How Easily He Forgets Racism," *Daily News* (New York), February 23, 2007. Democratic Party news release, "College Republicans Continue Racist, Anti-Immigrant Activities in Idaho," March 23, 2007. http://www.democrats.org/a/2007/03/college_republi_1.php

21 Massimo Calabresi, "Is Racism Fueling the Immigration Debate?" *Time*, May 17, 2006. http://www.time.com/time/nation/article/0,8599,1195250,00.html

22 Diego A. Santos, "Ex-Mexico Prez: Racists Stop Immigration," Associated Press, October 8, 2007.

http://www.breitbart.com/article.php?id=d8s5d6v80&show_article=1

## Point: Too Much Legal Immigration Is Damaging America's Economy and Society

1  Sanford Nowlin, "High-Tech Hardships: Squeezed out by Guest Workers?," *San Antonio Express-News*, May 4, 2003.

2  "Shameful H-1B Abuses" cited on the NIV Information Center Web site. http://www.zazona.com/ShameH1B/Abuses.htm

3  Kelly Jefferys and Randall Monger "Annual Flow Report: U.S. Legal Permanent Residents: 2007," Department of Homeland Security: Office of Immigration Statistics, March 2008. http://www.dhs.gov/xlibrary/assets/statistics/publications/LPR_FR_2007.pdf

4  Federation for American Immigration Reform, "Chain Migration" fact sheet. http://www.fairus.org/site/PageServer?pagename=iic_immigrationissuecenters3e2a

5  Stephen A. Camarota, "Immigrants in the United States, 2007: A Profile of America's Foreign-Born Population," Center for Immigration Studies, November 2007. http://www.cis.org/articles/2007/back1007.html

6  Ibid. U.S. Census Bureau, "Population Projections." http://www.census.gov/ipc/www/usinterimproj

7  Federation for American Immigration Reform. "Chain Migration" fact sheet.

8  "Immigration and Welfare," FAIR factsheet. http://www.fairus.org/site/PageServer?pagename=iic_immigrationissuecenters7fd8

9  Norman Matloff, "A Critical Analysis of the Economic Impacts of Immigration," July 1, 1995. http://www.cs.ucdavis.edu/~matloff/pub/Immigration/EconImpact/EconNM.html

10 Mark Krikorian and Steven A. Camarota, "Immigration and Terrorism: What is to Be Done?" Center for Immigration Studies Backgrounder, November 2001. http://www.cis.org/articles/2001/back1601.html

11 Karen Lee Scrivo, "Congress Probing Links Between Immigration, Terrorism," *CongressDaily*, March 10, 2003.

NOTES

http://www.govexec.com/dailyfed/0303/ 031003cd1.htm

12 Terence Chea, "Rival Factions Vie for Sierra Club Control," Associated Press, February 17, 2004.

13 Support U.S. Population Stabilization, "Global and Local Solutions to Population Growth" fact sheet. http://www.susps.org/overview/solutions.html

## Counterpoint: Immigrants Are a Vital Economic and Social Asset to the United States

1 Mary Laney, "Immigrant's Supermarket Success Story an Inspiration," *Chicago Sun-Times*, January 29, 2004.

2 Francis A. Walker, "Restriction of Immigration," *Atlantic Monthly*, June 1896. http://www.theatlantic.com/unbound/flashbks/immigr/walke.htm

3 Stephen A. Camarota, "Immigrants in the United States, 2007: A Profile of America's Foreign-Born Population," Center for Immigration Studies, November 2007. http://www.cis.org/articles/2007/back1007.html

4 *Cato Handbook for Congress: Policy Recommendations for the 108th Congress.* Washington, DC: Cato Institute, 2003, p. 632.

5 National Immigration Forum, "Top 10 Immigration Myths and Facts," June 2003. http://www.immigrationforum.org/documents/TheJourney/MythsandFacts.pdf

6 Historical information about the Red Scare can be found at http://www.spartacus.schoolnet.co.uk/USAredscare.htm

7 Phillip Ruthven, presentation to the 1990 National Immigration Outlook Conference, quoted in Lisa MacDonald, "Environment: Why Cutting Immigration Won't Help," *Green Left Weekly* (Australia), November 27, 1996. http://www.greenleft.org.au/back/1996/256/256cen.htm

8 U.S. Census Bureau statistics, 1990. http://www.census.gov/population/censusdata/90den_stco.txt

9 Mario Cuomo, "Immigration is Source of Our Strength," *USA Today*, July 19, 1993.

## Point: English Should Be the Official Language of the United States

1 "County Needs a Klingon Speaker," Associated Press, May 11, 2003. http://www.cnn.com/2003/US/West/05/10/offbeat.klingon.interpreter/index.html

2 Quoted in "Klingon in Oregon Update," "The Corner" blog on *National Review*, May 13, 2003. http://www.nationalreview.com/thecorner/03_05_11_corner-archive.asp#008534

3 Kimberly Melton, "Agencies Seek Interpreters," *Akron Beacon Journal*, July 7, 2003.

4 Paul von Zielbauer, "Hartford Bids a Bilingual Goodbye to a White-Collar Past," *New York Times*, May 5, 2003.

5 U.S. English, "Facts and Figures." http://www.us-english.org/inc/official/factsfigs.asp

6 Peter J. Duignan, "Bilingual Education: A Critique," cited on the Hoover Institution Web site. http://www.hoover.org/publications/he/2896386.html

7 James Crawford, "The English Only Movement," *Language Policy* Web site. http://ourworld.compuserve.com/homepages/JWCRAWFORD/engonly.htm

8 B.R. Chiswick and P.W. Miller, "Language in the Immigrant Labor Market," *Immigration, Language, and Ethnicity: Canada and the United States*, ed., Barry R. Chiswick. Washington, D.C.: American Enterprise Institute: 1992.

9 Tom Ramstack, "Labor Program Trains Hispanics in Job Safety," *Washington Times*, June 10, 2003.

10 Erin N. Marcus, "When a Patient Is Lost in the Translation," *New York Times*, April 8, 2003.

11 Duignan, "Bilingual Education: A Critique." http://www.hoover.org/publications/he/2896386.html

12 Quoted in Kathryn Jean Lopez, "Such a Lovely Place," *National Review*, June 11, 2003. http://www.nationalreview.com/interrogatory/interrogatory061103.asp

13 Quoted in http://www.proenglish.org/issues/offeng/index.html.

## Counterpoint: It Is Unnecessary to Have an Official Language

1 Quoted in *We are Bilingual: Essays from the 1982–2000 National Association for Bilingual Education Nationwide Writing Contest for Bilingual Students*. http://www.ncela.gwu.edu/pubs/nabe/essays/wearebilingual.pdf

2 James Crawford, "Demographic Change and Language," *Language Policy* Web site. http://ourworld.compuserve.com/homepages/JWCRAWFORD/can-pop.htm

3 John Adams, "Proposal for an American Language Academy," 1780, cited on *Language Policy* Web site. http://ourworld.compuserve.com/homepages/JWCRAWFORD/Adams.htm

4 "Ten Common Fallacies about Bilingual Education." http://www.ericdigests.org/1999-3/ten.htm

5 James Crawford, "Multilingual Government." http://ourworld.compuserve.com/homepages/JWCRAWFORD/can-mult.htm

6 Statistics from "ACLU Backgrounder on English Only Policies in Congress," American Civil Liberties Union briefing paper, December 10, 2007. http://www.aclu.org/immigrants/workplace/33092leg20071210.html

7 Cynthia Deike-Sims, "In the Battle Over English, Two Sides Enter Swinging," *True North* (Alaska), Spring 1999.

8 "ACLU Backgrounder on English Only Policies in Congress," http://www.aclu.org/immigrants/workplace/33092leg20071210.html

9 Ben Chandler, "Another Victory in the Fight Against Anti-Immigrant Ordinances," "Blog of Rights" blog on American Civil Liberties Union Web site, May 29, 2008. http://blog.aclu.org/2008/05/29/another-victory-in-the-fight-against-anti-immigrant-ordinances

10 U.S. Equal Employment Opportunity Commission, "EEOC Settles English-Only Suit for $2.44 Million Against University of Incarnate Word," news release, April 20, 2001. http://www.eeoc.gov/press/4-20-01.html

## Conclusion: The Future of Immigration Policy

1 Richard Boudreaux and Maura Reynolds, "Bush-Fox Talks Yield Easing of Travel, Work Rules," *Los Angeles Times*, March 7, 2004.

2 Quoted in "Asylum and Refugee Status" fact sheet. http://www.usvisa-law.com/immigration-asylum.htm

3 Eugene McCarthy, *A Colony of the World*, quoted in Federation for American Immigration Reform "What to Do About Refugees?" fact sheet, February 2003. http://www.fairus.org/site/PageServer?pagename=iic_immigrationissuecenters1314

4 Dalia Hashad, quoted in "As Immigrant Registration Deadlines Loom Once Again, ACLU Sees Trap for Arabs and Muslims," ACLU news release, October 30, 2003. http://www.aclu.org/safefree/general/18409prs20031030.html

# RESOURCES Ⅲ▷

## General

Bischoff, Henry. *Immigration Issues.* Westport, CT: Greenwood Press, 2002.

Daniels, Roger. *Guarding the Golden Door: American Immigration Policy and Immigrants Since 1882.* New York: Hill and Wang, 2004.

Graham, Otis. *Unguarded Gates: A History of America's Immigration Crisis.* Lanham, MD: Rowman & Littlefield, 2004.

LeMay, Michael. *U.S. Immigration: A Reference Handbook.* Santa Barbara, CA: ABC-CLIO, 2004.

Schuck, Peter. *Citizens, Strangers, and In-Betweens: Essays on Immigration and Citizenship.* Boulder, CO: Westview Press, 1998.

Wepman, Dennis. *Immigration: From the Founding of Virginia to the Closing of Ellis Island.* New York: Facts on File, 2002.

## Web Sites

**The American Civil Liberties Union (ACLU) on Immigrant Rights**
*http://www.aclu.org/ImmigrantsRights/Immigrants/index.html*
Explains the ACLU's position as a leading advocate for immigrants, refugees, and noncitizens.

**Federation for American Immigration Reform (FAIR)**
*http://www.fairus.org*
National nonprofit membership organization dedicated to protecting national interests by reforming immigration policies.

**National Immigration Forum**
*http://www.immigrationforum.org*
Forum committed to building support for public policies that welcome and protect immigrants.

**U.S. Citizenship and Immigration Services (USCIS)**
*http://uscis.gov/portal/site/uscis*
Official site of the government bureau within the Department of Homeland Security that manages immigration services. Web site includes information laws, forms, services, and programs related to citizenship and immigration.

## Illegal Immigration

Condon, Bradly J., and Tapen Sinha. *Drawing Lines in Sand and Snow: Border Security and North American Economic Integration.* Armonk, NY: M.E. Sharpe, 2003.

Ehrenreich, Rosa. *Slipping Through the Cracks: Unaccompanied Children Detained by the U.S. Immigration and Naturalization Service.* New York: Human Rights Watch, 1997.

Haines, David, and Karen Rosenblum, eds. *Illegal Immigration in America: A Reference Handbook.* Westport, CT: Greenwood Press, 1999.

Ngai, Mae. *Impossible Subjects: Illegal Aliens and the Making of Modern America.* Princeton, NJ: Princeton University Press, 2004.

Yoshida, Chisato. *Illegal Immigration and Economic Welfare.* Heidelberg, Germany: Physica-Verlag, 2000.

### Web Sites

**National Network for Immigrant and Refugee Rights**
*http://www.nnirr.org*
National organization of coalitions and activists working to protect immigrants and refugees by promoting just policies and defending their rights.

## Border Fence

Andreas, Peter. *Border Games: Policing the U.S.-Mexico Divide.* Ithaca, NY: Cornell University Press, 2000.

Danelo, David. *The Border: Exploring the U.S.-Mexican Divide.* Mechanicsburg, PA: Stackpole Books, 2008.

Romero, Fernando. *Hyperborder: The Contemporary U.S.-Mexico Border and Its Future.* New York: Princeton Architectural Press, 2007.

### Web Sites

**Border Fence Project**
*http://www.borderfenceproject.com*
Citizens group organized to facilitate building of the border fence through private donations and volunteer work.

**Department of Homeland Security Border Fence Sections**
*http://www.dhs.gov/xprevprot/programs/border-fence-southwest.shtm*
DHS fact page explaining the various boundaries on the U.S.-Mexico border.

**No Texas Border Wall**
*http://www.notexasborderwall.com*
Grassroots coalition of groups and individuals concerned about the border fence and working to repeal the Secure Fence Act and REAL ID Act.

# RESOURCES ⫼▷

## Legal Immigration

Bean, Frank, and Gillian Stevens. *America's Newcomers and the Dynamics of Diversity.* New York: Russell Sage Foundation, 2003.

Eldredge, Dirk Chase. *Crowded Land of Liberty: Solving America's Immigration Crisis.* Bridgehampton, NY: Bridge Works, 2001.

Gunderson, Theodore, ed. *Immigration Policy in Turmoil.* New York: Nova Science Publishers, 2002.

Magana, Lisa. *Straddling the Border: Immigration Policy and the INS.* Austin, TX: University of Texas Press, 2004.

Massey, Douglas. *Beyond Smoke and Mirrors: Mexican Immigration in an Era of Economic Integration.* New York: Russell Sage Foundation, 2002.

### Web Sites
**Jobs and Immigration (Cato Institute)**
*http://www.freetrade.org/issues/immigration.html*
Site maintained by the Cato Institute, a libertarian think tank, that features articles and studies in favor of immigration.

**"The New Americans" (PBS Series)**
*http://www.pbs.org/newamericans/*
Companion Web site to PBS documentary program following the lives of new Americans in the twenty-first century.

## "English Only" Laws

Baron, Dennis. *The English-Only Question: An Official Language for Americans?* New Haven, CT: Yale University Press, 1990.

Del Valle, Sandra. *Language Rights and the Law in the United States: Finding Our Voices.* Buffalo, NY: Multilingual Matters, 2003.

Piatt, Bill. *Only English?: Law and Language Policy in the United States.* Albuquerque: University of New Mexico Press, 1990.

Tse, Lucy. *"Why Don't They Learn English?": Separating Fact from Fallacy in the U.S. Language Debate.* New York: Teachers College Press, 2001.

## *Web Sites*

### English First
*http://www.englishfirst.org*
Nonprofit lobbying organization founded to promote English as America's official language and to eliminate multilingual policies.

### National Association for Bilingual Education
*http://www.nabe.org*
Nonprofit organization dedicated to promoting educational excellence and equity for English language learners.

# PICTURE CREDITS ⫻▷

## PAGE

**ALAN ALLPORT** was born in Whiston, England, and grew up in East Yorkshire. He has a master's degree in history from the University of Pennsylvania and is currently a Ph.D. candidate at that institution, with a special interest in nineteenth- and twentieth-century European history. He is writing a dissertation on the experience of World War II veterans. He lives in Philadelphia with his partner, Barbara, and their son, Thomas.

**JOHN E. FERGUSON JR.** teaches negotiation in the Hankamer School of Business at Baylor University in Waco, Texas. As a constitutional attorney and scholar, he has provided mediation and training to public schools and communities in 34 states. He earned his Masters of Theological Studies and J.D. degrees from Vanderbilt University's Divinity and Law Schools and is a member of the Tennessee, Washington, D.C., and United States Supreme Court bars.

**ALAN MARZILLI, M.A., J.D.,** lives in Washington, D.C., and is a program associate with Advocates for Human Potential, Inc., a research and consulting firm based in Sudbury, Mass., and Albany, N.Y. He primarily works on developing training and educational materials for agencies of the federal government on topics such as housing, mental health policy, employment, and transportation. He has spoken on mental health issues in 30 states, the District of Columbia, and Puerto Rico; his work has included training mental health administrators, nonprofit management and staff, and people with mental illnesses and their families on a wide variety of topics, including effective advocacy, community-based mental health services, and housing. He has written several handbooks and training curricula that are used nationally and as far away as the territory of Guam. Additionally, he managed statewide and national mental health advocacy programs and worked for several public interest lobbying organizations while studying law at Georgetown University. He has written more than a dozen books, including numerous titles in the POINT/COUNTERPOINT series.